JUST LIVING

JUST

COLUMBIA UNIVERSITY PRESS / NEW YORK

LIVING

POEMS AND PROSE BY THE
JAPANESE MONK TONNA

Edited and Translated by Steven D. Carter

Columbia University Press wishes to express its appreciation for assistance given by the Humanities Center of the University of California, Irvine, and the Dean's Office of the University of California, Irvine, toward the cost of publishing this book.

COLUMBIA UNIVERSITY PRESS
Publishers Since 1893
New York   Chichester, West Sussex
Copyright © 2003 Columbia University Press
All rights reserved

Library of Congress Cataloging-in-Publication Data

Ton'a, 1289?–1372?
[Selections. 2002]
Just living : poems and prose by the Japanese monk Tonna /
edited and translated by Steven D. Carter
p. cm. — (Translations from the Asian classics)
Includes bibliographical references and index.
ISBN 0-231-12552-6 (cloth : alk. paper)
ISBN 0-231-12553-4 (paper : alk. paper)
I. Carter, Steven D. II. Title. III. Series.

PL792.T64 A6 2002
895.6'122—dc21   2002067669

♾

Columbia University Press books are printed on
permanent and durable acid-free paper.
Printed in the United States of America
Designed by Lisa Hamm
c 10 9 8 7 6 5 4 3 2 1
p 10 9 8 7 6 5 4 3 2 1

To Kimberley

Contents

Acknowledgments

As always, I thank my wife, Mary, for her support. Thanks are also due two anonymous readers for Columbia University Press whose suggestions did much to improve the manuscript.

During the fall of 1999, I was able to spend four months at the National Institute of Japanese Literature in Tokyo as a research fellow, working on the translations presented in this book as well as other research projects. I thank the faculty and staff of the institute, particularly Director Matsuno Yōichi and Professors Robert Campbell, Matsumura Yūji, Asada Tōru, Kuboki Hideo, and Horikawa Takashi, for their support and assistance. While at the institute, I also benefited greatly from the insights of Iwasa Miyoko, Araki Hisashi, Itō Kei, and other Japanese scholars who attended my Tonna seminar. Needless to say, any mistakes in interpretation are mine and mine alone.

For financial assistance toward the publication of the book, I thank the Humanities Center and Dean Karen Lawrence of the School of Humanities, University of California, Irvine.

JUST LIVING

Introduction

ᛰ

One wonders what sort of answer one would get from Japanese scholars today to the question of who was the finest poet of the Japanese *uta* form. The mid–Edo period poet-scholar Mushanokōji Sanekage was unequivocal about the subject: "One should continually ponder the masterworks of the poets of the past," he said, "and among these it is the poems of Tonna most of all that one should continually savor."[1]

Of course, Sanekage was not a modern reader. In fact, he was probably not thinking about readers at all, modern or otherwise, when he made his comment, but rather about young poets—producers rather than merely consumers of the art. That he chose not an earlier master such as Saigyō or Fujiwara no Shunzei or his son Teika but Tonna (1289–1372) is noteworthy, however, especially when one realizes how neglected the works of Tonna have been by mainstream Japanese scholarship. The modern Japanese academic establishment has concentrated so much on earlier periods of literature that poets writing after the Shinkokin age (1180–1225) have generally gotten short shrift. It is also true that Tonna has often been attacked simply because he was a conspicuous target for anyone reacting against the old traditions he was unfailingly adduced to represent. For whatever reason, assaults against him have seldom been true critiques based on a careful reading of his work, the importance of which is hard to deny in either historical or artistic terms.

There is no disputing that the Shinkokin age was a golden one for the *uta*. Yet the continuing importance of that ancient form in elite culture for the next three hundred years should not be overlooked. Long after the death of Teika, his progeny in various lineages and their scores of students continued to produce exemplary work in the genre, which over time also gained adherents among the military elite. At court, then, but also in the houses of great warlords, the *uta* was pursued as an avocation via poetry gatherings and contests and the compilation of anthologies in the manner of earlier poets. Furthermore, during these years the *uta* was more than ever before a part of social life among those in positions of power, whether at court, in the halls of military institutions, or in Buddhist monasteries and Shinto shrines. Many social events—celebrations, votive and memorial services, dedications, and so on—virtually required the composition of poems; and on less formal occasions the ability to compose a proper poem of felicitation, greeting, or condolence was a useful, if not necessary, talent. Among other things, this meant that there was a need for masters of the art who could teach it as a craft to younger poets. Tonna was, first and foremost, one of these masters, who pursued his art as a professional poet in a lively cultural market.

Tonna was born into a high-ranking military family, the Nikaidō, in 1289, most likely in Kyōto. About his father, Nikaidō Mitsusada, we know little except that he served for a time as a provincial governor. Whether his son was trained for an administrative career or not, the records do not say, but we can ascertain that by his early twenties he had taken the tonsure as a lay monk and was studying at Enryakuji, the Tendai monastery on Mount Hiei. For the younger sons of prominent families who could never hope to displace their older brothers as heirs to family offices and titles, the priesthood offered both a living and a measure of social respectability. Furthermore, Buddhist monasteries were artistic and intellectual centers that offered young men of talent a way into the cultural elite. Tonna (also pronounced Ton'a)—which is the religious name by which he would be known—doubtlessly was such a young man.

Tonna would remain a lay monk all his life but would never hold ecclesiastical office. Records associate him in particular with the Ji, or "Time," sect, which for complex historical reasons was favored by commoner artists of all sorts, especially poets, gardeners, dramatists, and, later, tea masters. It is fairly clear, then, that from early on Tonna dedicated himself to the Way of poetry, which he thought of as a Buddhist way toward enlightenment as well. Many poets of the past who were from similar backgrounds—most prominently, Saigyō, whom he looked to as a mentor—had walked the same path. For Tonna, then, *keiko,* or "composition practice," would be something akin to a devotional, as well as professional, activity, as important in and of itself as the poems he produced in the process.

To pursue the Way of poetry in Japan in the fourteenth century required, first of all, study under an acknowledged master who could provide both instruction and the social introductions that were necessary for entrée into the elite society that was the only arena for poetic recognition and success. In Tonna's case, the master turned out to be Nijō Tameyo, head of the senior branch of the Mikohidari lineage at the imperial court. For some time, the Nijō house had cultivated close relationships with the warrior elite, who were always ready to enhance their social profiles by participation in artistic activities and who offered considerable wealth and resources in gratitude for artistic services. The other prominent Mikohidari house, the Kyōgoku, was so dominated by high-ranking courtiers and members of the imperial family that it was probably not within the reach of a man of such humble status. For these reasons, and no doubt other ones that remain unknown to us, Tonna became a disciple of Tameyo, under whom he studied composition and to whom he submitted work for scrutiny. By 1320 Tonna had so impressed his teacher that he was even given the house's "secret teachings" on the *Kokinshū* (Collection of ancient and modern times, 905) and other early poetic works, which soon allowed him to put out his own shingle as a master of poetry.[2] Before long, he was taking on disciples and students of his own and engaging in the accepted activities of his profession—correcting students' work, collecting manuscripts, writing commentaries, lecturing on the classics, and of course organizing and supervising poetry gatherings at his own cottage and at the homes of patrons. We know of at least half a dozen other commoner masters in Kyōto at the time engaged in similar activities. Tonna would soon reign supreme among them.

For the next fifty years, Tonna was a fixture in the capital, through good times and bad. When the Nijō house went through lean years during the ascendancy of the Kyōgoku house and their patrons in the Jimyō'in imperial lineage, Tonna remained loyal; in return, when the Nijō house dominated poetic circles, as it did for most of the time, he benefited. By the mid-1340s, records indicate, Tonna— along with other notable monk-poets, such as Yoshida no Kenkō, author of the famous miscellany *Tsurezuregusa* (Essays in idleness)—was polishing his craft as one of a select group of participants in Nijō poetry meetings, which were held three times monthly.[3] Living in cottages in various areas on the outskirts of the capital, he seems to have enjoyed a comfortable existence. Tonna's patrons among the military families no doubt paid him well for his services as master of ceremonies at their poetic gatherings, and it may be that he also had some income from his family. In any case, records make it clear that he was a man of great social, as well as artistic, gifts—no aloof recluse but a *suki,* or recognized devotee of the arts.

But even for a monk like Tonna, poetry, especially Japanese poetry in the *uta* form, was a courtly form the practice of which required specialized knowledge and, ultimately, a courtly pedigree, or at least strong courtly affiliations. Through hard work, Tonna gained the last. However, he could never supplant his teachers of the Mikohidari bloodline. No one of commoner status could hope to attain the social prominence of the Nijō masters, on whose political and ideological support Tonna was more or less dependent. Thus when imperial anthologies of the genre were issued— and seven of them were compiled during his long career— he could never hope for more than a few of his poems to be included; and on formal occasions he could never truly take center stage, instead always deferring to his superiors in birth, however inferior some of them may have been in terms of talent. By the 1350s, however, it is clear that he was highly respected by even the leaders of the courtly factions. His personal anthologies and other sources indicate that he could number among his patrons the Ashikaga shoguns Takauji and Yoshiakira, other prominent military figures such as Utsunomiya Sadayasu and Saitō Mototō, several imperial princes, courtiers of the highest rank such as the regent Nijō Yoshimoto (of the regental Nijō family, not to be confused with the poetic lineage of the same name), and clerics of all ranks too numerous to mention. In a sense, his Nijō teachers were also patrons in that they made a place for him in their activities and sanctioned his work as part of their tradition.

The mid-fourteenth century was a time of great political upheaval: the rebellion of Emperor Go-Daigo, the fall of the Hōjō family and the establishment of the Ashikaga shogunate, and conflicts associated with the warring Northern and Southern Courts—the last beginning in the 1330s and continuing into the next century. Tonna, of course, experienced and lived through these conflicts. Occasionally, he

even wrote poems that hint at his sadness over endless battles
that never seemed to result in an age of peace (poem 78):

WRITTEN AT HIS NINNAJI COTTAGE

A sad thing it is
to hear it
            in company
with the world's woes—
a storm
            in the mountains
so near
            to the capital.[4]

yo no usa o / soete kiku koso / kanashikere
miyako ni chikaki / yama no arashi ni

Just which of the "woes" of the time he is referring to
in this poem we do not know. Battles broke out near the
capital, and even within its precincts, many times during his
life. It must be said, though, that for a devout Buddhist such
happenings were simply the way of the world: the annals of
the past told a bloody story. Like most of those not directly
involved in conflicts, Tonna thus tried to stay aloof, following
the dictum of Teika many years before: "Red banners and
chastising rebels are no concern of mine."[5] And the same
attitudes evidently characterized his life as an artist, as evi-
denced by the fact that he was also able to maintain working
relationships with four generations of Nijō poets despite con-
stant infighting and intrigue within their ranks. As a monk
with some financial independence, Tonna seems to have been
able to remain above politics most of the time, mixing safely
with members of warring factions, political or otherwise. In
his last decades, he even had cordial relations with the cour-
tier Reizei Tamehide, a member of another lineage of the
Mikohidari house that was generally hostile to Nijō interests.

It goes without saying that there was no "publishing" of literary works in fourteenth-century Japan, at least in the modern sense of the word. Only Buddhist sutras were available in woodblock form, and Japanese court poetry, in particular, was so bound up with the art of calligraphy and so much an artistic tradition in its own right that to reduce it to the impersonality of print would have seemed a sacrilege. In his own day, those who knew Tonna's work knew it only through word of mouth or handwritten records of the many poetic events—such as hundred-poem sequences, poem contests, and votive offerings to shrines—in which he participated. As preparations were under way for an imperial anthology in the late 1350s, however, the poet began to put together a personal anthology of his poems, titled *Tonna hōshi ei* (Poems by Monk Tonna).[6] From its pages, Nijō Tamesada chose four poems for inclusion in the imperial anthology (*Shin senzaishū* [The new collection of a thousand years], 1359)—a modest number, it would seem, but equal to the number accorded his late colleague Jōben. As noted before, *jige kajin* (commoner poets without court rank) could never hope to receive the attention their courtly counterparts received in such venues. Yoshida no Kenkō was represented by only three poems, while Jōben's son, Keiun (precise dates unknown), was passed over entirely.

Not long after the appearance of the new imperial anthology, Tonna compiled a more substantial collection of his work to date, to which he gave the title *Sōanshū* (The grass hut collection). It contained 1,446 poems, divided, like virtually all poetic works of the time, into books on the four seasons, love, and miscellaneous topics. Soon it was widely circulated as a compendium of poems that could serve as models for aspiring poets hoping to master the *uta* form. So by 1360 Tonna had truly arrived as a master. Sometime before, he had built a cottage near Ninnaji that he called the Saike'en (White Lotus Garden), a very substantial residence surrounded by gardens with the finest plants from famous places all around Japan—plums from Naniwa, cherry trees from Yoshino, bush clover from Miyagino, maples from Mount Tatsuta, and creeping vines from Mount Utsu. There he hosted poetic gatherings for his friends and patrons and by about 1366 produced another personal anthology, *Zoku Sōanshū* (The grass hut anthology, continued), that contained poems not included in the earlier works, as well as works from more recent years. Now regarded as the preeminent *jige* master of the art, he was evidently in great demand as both teacher and lecturer. So impressed by his work was the imperial regent and literatus Nijō Yoshimoto that the latter penned a work based on questions he had asked the patriarch, which he titled *Gumon kenchū* (Wise answers to foolish questions, 1363). Not long after, Tonna put together his own most comprehensive pedagogical work, *Seiashō* (Notes of a frog at the bottom of the well), in which he copied for his students important passages from earlier works by masters of the past on a variety of topics, adding a few comments of his own and a section of chatty anecdotes, bits of lore, and advice (*zōdan*) from his own experience over the years.

Tonna's greatest public honor came in 1364, when he was asked to complete the work of compiling the next imperial anthology (*Shin shūishū* [New collection of gleanings]) after the untimely death late in that year of the man acting as chief compiler, Nijō Tameakira. Never before had one without court rank been trusted with such a task. Although he accepted the job with some trepidation, Tonna finished the work—which Tameakira had left about half done— speedily, offering the completed anthology for review several months after receiving his charge. The final product received criticism from some quarters for including too many of his own poems (nine; ten, counting one entered as anonymous; and eleven, counting one that is quoted in the headnote to another poem) and too many poems by monks and military men in the sections he had put together. However, the shogun, Ashikaga Yoshiakira, who was by this time studying under Tonna, was pleased, as were the young heirs of the Nijō lineage for whom Tonna was clearly an avuncular figure of considerable poetic authority.

Obviously, association with the most prestigious of poetic endeavors improved Tonna's standing even more in the cultural community of his time. For one thing, serving as compiler gave him access to various secret Mikohidari documents concerning the proper handling of such tasks—knowledge that gave the monk-poet a kind of cultural capital usually denied those of commoner status. Still, he could not serve as master at court affairs; that was a task reserved for young members of the Nijō and Reizei lineages with the proper pedigrees. But his many honors and the treasured teachings that came along with them did make it possible for him to set up a separate poetic lineage of his own that would continue for more than a century after his death. This descended through his son Kyōken, eventually to Gyōkō of the Jōkō'in cloister near Saike'en at Ninnaji, where the heirs of the line held sway with the title Dharma Sign and the office of bishop. Records also indicate that, beginning in Kyōken's time, Tonna's heirs held the title of superintendent (*bettō*) of Niitamatsushima Shrine, a Shintō shrine located in Kyōto (first on Fifth Avenue, then at Saike'en and on First Avenue, and finally back to Ninnaji in Gyōkō's time) that was specifically dedicated to the god of poetry.[7] All these appointments involved incomes, of course, which helped solidify the place of Tonna's heirs in court culture. With such finances to support it, the Saike'en would go on to become one of the most famous gardens in the capital, attracting visitors as prominent as the Ashikaga shoguns.[8]

Tonna's honors rubbed a number of his social "betters" the wrong way. Within a few decades after his death, Imagawa Ryōshun, a military man who could boast court rank and a partisan of the Reizei lineage, complained that he could not understand why people looked up to Tonna as if he were "some kind of sage of poetry."[9] In the main, though, later generations extolled him as precisely that. The next imperial anthology, compiled after his death in 1383, with a preface by Tonna's friend and student Nijō Yoshimoto, included eight of Tonna's poems; and the one after that, for which his descendant Gyōkō served as librarian, included nineteen. His stock continued to rise into the Edo period, finally resulting in the reputation noted at the beginning of this introduction.

Tonna's poetic attitudes are usually characterized as conservative, and there is some truth in the characterization: he was a believer in carrying on the poetic traditions of the imperial court and rather dismissive of anything that could be described as unorthodox. This does not mean, however, that he was rigid and uncompromising. Indeed, his very existence as a master operating in a social arena depended on the ability to act as a mediator. If anything, he was therefore a practicer of the "middle way"—which he encouraged, especially in his less gifted students, as the safest route to acceptance in social circles. In this sense, on pedagogical issues he is perhaps best described as a moderate who believed in teaching his students a craft that could be relied on rather than a mysterious "art" that demanded imponderables, such as inspiration and creativity, that could probably not be taught in any case. And it also must be said that his was a society in which powers of memory were more important than powers of originality. The exhibition of knowledge and mastery of technique (that is, the exercise of imagination within accepted conventions) counted for more in a social setting than flights of fancy.

To properly understand Tonna's critical works, one must therefore remember that they were written primarily for beginning students who wanted concrete direction on the practice of poetry in a very particular setting. To properly understand his poetry, one must further keep in mind that it was almost all produced in social situations, requiring a thorough knowledge of the canon and rhetorical skill above all else. The headnotes to his poems show that he was a constant participant in monthly poetry gatherings at the homes of patrons, in poem contests, and in commissioned sequences—all formal venues in which work had to be produced according to strict precedents. Of course, such events required the exercise of imagination, too, although an imagination exercised only within prescribed limits. A poet in such a setting might be compared with a gymnast or figure skater whose task is to work various required skills into a performance that seems effortless but in fact is the product of long hours of preparation and training. Like other poets, Tonna aimed to impress, but less with flashes of creativity than with subtlety and wit—with compulsory skills and, if possible, a little more.

One of these "compulsory skills" was the rhetorical technique of *honkadori* (allusive variation)—the explicit borrowing of lines from an earlier poem to provide the framework for one's own. In the hands of some poets, the technique led to mere repetition. Ideally, though, the aim was to use the technique to enter into a sort of dialogue with an earlier text, producing not a copy but a true variation, as in this example from late in Tonna's life:

ON "BLOSSOMS AT A BARRIER GATE,"
WRITTEN WHEN THE DANSHŌ PRINCE
VISITED SAIKE'EN, AT A TIME WHEN THE
BLOSSOMS WERE IN FULL BLOOM

At Meeting Hill,
the guards
            who bar the way
can relax a while—
their task of halting
                        passersby
left
      to the cherry blossoms.[10]

ausaka no / seki no sekimori / itoma are ya
hito o todomuru / hana ni makasete

Taken by itself, this is a witty poem in praise of cherry blossoms so alluring that they perform the task of "stopping" travelers on the road when they come to the famous toll barrier at Ausaka, Meeting Hill. Those with Tonna in his cottage when the poem was composed, however, would also have recognized an allusion to a poem from *Shin kokinshū* by the twelfth-century poet Shōmyō, on an entirely different topic, "Seedlings in the Rain":

> When the rain comes down,
> the men working
> > in the fields
> can relax a while—
>
> their task of flooding
> > seedling beds
> left
> > to the sky above.[11]

> *ame fureba / oda no masurao / itoma are ya*
> *nawashiromizu o / sora ni makasete*

Beyond elevating a scene of labor (farmers working in rice paddies) into the realm of the aesthetic (travelers "detained" by cherry blossoms), Tonna's poem does little in the way of semantics. Instead, it simply appropriates the earlier poem as a syntactic "shell" to be filled with new imagery. In doing so, however, it also serves the purpose of inviting those around him to appreciate a gesture intelligible only to those with special knowledge—thus reinforcing the "social bond" of a shared canon that perforce underlies notions of taste. Clearly, the ability to invoke poems of the past in this way was highly prized among poets at poetic gatherings. That Tonna used the technique in so many of his poems is evidence not of a lack of creativity but, on the contrary, of his mastery of the art of composition in his own literary field.

By all accounts, Tonna was indeed a master of the *za,* or composition venue—at his own home or at the homes of patrons or disciples, wherever poetry was composed in a social setting. Typically, conventional topics (*dai*) for poetic gatherings were handed out ahead of time, but almost always an event ended with extemporaneous composition, a talent for which was virtually required for success as a master. And it was here that Tonna evidently shone above most others of his time, as a later professional poet notes:

> At a poetry gathering attended by Tamehide along with Ton'a, Keiun, Jōben, and Kenkō—celebrated poets of the day known as the Four Guardian Kinds of Japanese poetry—each of these last chose six topics on which to compose his poems, while Tamehide chose even more. The participants of lower rank who were still novices in the art chose one or two topics apiece. Now Ton'a, having glanced through his six topics, said, "I must excuse myself for a short time. I shall be back as soon as I am free." And depositing his six topic slips under a shelf at the side of the room, he went out. Thereupon, Keiun substituted his own six topics for those that Ton'a had left.
>
> In due course, when everyone had composed his poems and written them down to be passed in, and people were asked what could be keeping him, Ton'a came back. Picking up the topics he had left behind, he ground some ink and prepared to write his poems, only to discover that these were not his topics, all six of them proving on examination to be different from the topics he had originally chosen. Even so, not a bit flustered, he said, "Well, someone has been playing a trick on me, I see. Who did it?" And he continued to grind his ink, dip in his brush, and quickly write down six poems, one right after the other.
>
> After the poems had been read out loud, Keiun said, "You performed most creditably. It is at a time like this that a poet's true mastery is revealed." Ton'a replied, "What an outrageous thing to have done! You, one of the senior poets,

who ought to have been warning the others not to play such tricks!"[12]

Shōtetsu, the poet who recorded this incident, was politically allied with Tonna's rivals in the Reizei lineage, yet his respect for the talents of a master working in the same arena is obvious. As Keiun says in the anecdote, Tonna's mastery was doubtlessly most evident at the moment of composition, as a kind of performance. It was for such a setting that he had been disciplined by his teachers; it was for such a setting that he trained his own students.

But how is a modern reader to make sense of poetry produced in such a setting? First, it should be said that many of Tonna's poems can be understood even now without any special knowledge. A poem like the following stands well on its own as a descriptive "nature" poem:

> Not at all
>   like snow
> so ready to melt away—
> these cherry blossoms
> fallen but then
>   lifted again
> by storm winds
>   in the garden.[13]

> *kiegate no / yuki to mo miezu / sakurabana*
> *tsumoreba harau / niwa no arashi ni*

To imagine the poet creating this scene after seeing cherry petals descending on a garden only to be blown into the air again by passing winds does this poem little harm. Only a true pedant would deny that even when viewed as straightforward description the scene has a certain appeal.

Yet our involvement with the poem is only enhanced when we approach it in a way that takes into account the way it was produced, in a particular poetic culture whose values were rather different from our own. As a first step toward moving in this direction, it is useful to begin with attention to things such as *honkadori* and *dai,* in contemplation of which almost all the poems of Tonna and his contemporaries were composed. Knowing that the poem was composed on the conventional topic "Fallen Blossoms," for instance, may add something to our appreciation of Tonna's mastery. In particular, that knowledge can help us catch the subtle new ways the poem deals with the *idea* of fallen blossoms. For at the time of its composition, the poem was probably not a description of any actual scene at all but the "treatment" of an idea—and a rather creative one. Many earlier poems had compared blossoms to snow, as many poems had depicted blossoms blown from the trees by storm winds; Tonna's accomplishment was to add to this the idea of "blossom flurries" created time and time again by winds after the blossoms have fallen. For those who first heard it at the poetic gathering for which it was composed, the tension of the poem must have turned on that point, and there is no reason that readers today—if properly prepared for the task—cannot experience the poem at least partly in the same way.

Dai, of course, had been in existence since long before Tonna's day. They had their origin in the early Heian period, when poems were first composed in poem contests, providing "common ground" on which poets could be judged. It was later on, in the late Heian period, when the composition of poem sequences had come to dominate poetic affairs, that *dai* were virtually enshrined as part of poetic discourse. The earliest examples were one-word topics, such as "spring," "summer," "autumn," "winter," "love," "travel," and so on— which also happened to be the major categories of imperial and other anthologies. In time, more complex varieties developed, involving phrases such as "Blossoms at Night" and "Love, with the Word 'Cloud' as an Image." By Tonna's time, one finds the whole range of topics in use, from one-word topics of the distant past to compound topics of relatively recent vintage. Almost never, however, was a poet able to concoct a topic entirely on his own.

Rather than titles that were attached to poems after the fact, *dai* were thus part of a conventional lexicon of the genre; and, in most cases, the poet did not even choose his own topics but received them from a participant charged with the task of choosing—generally from sanctioned lists—for the group. In this sense, the topic was therefore given to the poet exactly as an assignment or challenge. Generally speaking, the poem he produced had to contain the actual word or words of the topic. The task was to accomplish this within accepted rhetorical limits and to present the topic in a slightly new way. The topic "Fallen Blossoms," for instance, had been daunting poets for hundreds of years before Tonna ever confronted it. Compound topics such as "Cherry Blossoms at Night" were slightly less overworked but demanded the handling of more vocabulary.

One way for modern readers to understand Tonna's poems *in their otherness,* then, is to regard them as a master's response to the challenge presented by the *dai.* The first poem in the translations that follow is a good example of how Tonna measured up to the task. The headnote indicates that it was written at the Poetry Bureau, referring to the offices at court where the compilation of imperial anthologies and other formal business were undertaken. Exactly what sort of meeting took place is not mentioned. But we can be sure that at the bureau, the rituals would have been honored. Perhaps the poem was written beforehand on a topic that had been passed out (*kenjitsu*); perhaps it was composed on the spot (*tōza*). In either case, it would have been read aloud by the lector before the assembled group. And it was judged, first of all, on how well it dealt with its topic, in this case "Early Spring." Past precedent dictated that such a topic introduce images associated with both winter and spring in a way that showed movement toward the latter:

In fair Yoshino
the wind low
                    on the mountain slopes

grows more chilly still;
and half-hidden

              in the haze—
fine flakes of falling snow.[14]

miyoshino no / yama no shitakaze / nao saete
kasumigakure ni / awayuki zo furu

Tonna's poem succeeds well in doing what was expected on the occasion, depicting a scene that is the perfect blend of winter and spring imagery—snow and spreading haze. But this would be only routine for a master. No doubt what truly impressed his auditors was the wonderful contrast provided by the first and last lines of the poem, beginning with the lofty image of Yoshino—a storied place in southern Yamato Province famous for its rugged mountains and spectacular vistas—and ending with *awayuki*, "delicate flakes of snow." The occasion demanded nothing revolutionary but instead a poem of dignity and power, lofty in tone, which is exactly what the master produced.

In other venues, Tonna could be somewhat more adventurous, although always within the limits of decorum. The following poem on "Returning Geese," for example, is again on a conventional topic about which thousands of poems had already been produced. In this case, those present no doubt expected some variation on the usual treatment, which would involve some image of the geese fading off into the spring sky, making their way back to the continent for the summer. But in this poem, Tonna produced something slightly unexpected:

Even in
       a world
full of false promises
they will not
          forget

their pledge
                to come back home—
those geese now flying away.[15]

itsuwari no / aru yo ni dani mo / furusato no
chigiri wasurezu / kari no yukuran

Nijō Yoshimoto said of Tonna that his "cadences are pro-
found, his conceptions smooth and never overstated; and
there is something just a little different about each of his
poems that is felt by those around him in any gathering."[16]
This poem is a fine example of what Yoshimoto meant. Not
until the last line does the topic come in, a fact that must
have produced some suspense in the *za*. Indeed, the first lines
of the poem lead one to expect a love poem. But at the end,
Tonna pulls it together in another masterful performance.

    Not all of Tonna's poems were written on *dai*. The
headnote to the following poem, for instance, indicates that
it was written as truly "descriptive" of an actual experience:

WRITTEN WHEN SOME WATERFOWL
RAISED BY CHILDREN WERE RELEASED
INTO THE WATERS OF HIROSAWA POND
["BROAD POND"]

Accustomed by now
to life
        in the rocky narrows
of a garden stream,
broad, indeed,
                to the ducks
                        must seem
the waters of Broad Pond.[17]

yarimizu no / sebaki iwama ni / suminarete
sazo hirosawa no / ike no oshidori

That this poem is built around a pun makes it easy to identify as a courtly poem, as do its orthodox vocabulary and somewhat playful tone. To this extent, even without the presence of a mediating *dai*, it is a conventional work. Yet it shows that Tonna, however much a product of the discourse in which he operated, could be creative within its limits.

It should also be noted that despite his strong Nijō affiliations, Tonna did not write in only the style of "deep feeling" (*ushin*, for which the poem beginning "Even in a world . . ." may stand as an example), for which poets of that camp were known.[18] As noted previously, he had a cordial relationship with Reizei Tamehide of the competing Kyōgoku–Reizei faction, whose influence is apparent in poems like this one written at the cottage of Yoshida no Kenkō on the topic "The Late Autumn Moon":

> Through gaps in the clouds
> that drop showers
>   as they pass,
> the moonlight
>   spills down—
> fading quickly
>   into the dark
> of the dusky autumn sky.[19]

shigure suru / kumo no taema o / moru tsuki no
hayaku mo kururu / aki no sora kana

The emphasis on a moment of change in the natural scenery, the imagery of light and shadow, the attempt to push the "witnessing" subject into the background and let the scene appear "as it is" (*ari no mama*)—all these things are associated not with the Nijō house but with Kyōgoku Tamekane and his adherents. That Tonna produced a number of similar poems is evidence that he was above all a versatile master of the art. This is a point borne out even more so by some of the poems produced in his later years that have all the marks of the Song monochromatic aesthetic entering Japan through Zen monasteries, as evidenced in this example from *Zoku Sōanshū:*

"SNOW AT SHORESIDE"

A winter so cold
that the snow is
                    piling up
at harborside—
where
        left by the bank to rot
is a cast-off
            fishing boat.[20]

*fuyu samumi / yuki zo furitsumu / minatoe ni
kuchite nokoru / ama no sutebune*

Some years later, Shōtetsu—again, a devotee of the opposite political camp—would be criticized for producing precisely so stark a scene in one of his own poems.[21] That Tonna preceded him in doing so shows that the latter was no unbending conservative but very much a "practicing" poet.

This fact is also evident when one reads the anecdotes he recorded in the last book of *Seiashō,* a few of which are translated in this book. For the student of poetic history, these notes, recorded late in life, provide a gold mine of information about the poetic practice of the time, as well as biographical details about famous poets of the past—Tonna himself and his contemporaries. The most common recurrent theme is the central place of the master–disciple relationship in poetic affairs—perhaps a natural outcome for something written by a master. But the anecdotes also show how wide was his circle of patrons and friends, which included not only Nijō stalwarts such as Tameyo (the Late Master) and Tamefuji (the Minister of Popular Affairs) but also Reizei

Tamehide, numerous courtiers, warlords, and poet-priests like himself, many of whom were not directly affiliated with the factions of the time. This is not to suggest that the anecdotes reveal Tonna as something other than a Nijō partisan in most matters, which he most definitely was. It is to insist, however, that they reveal a man not completely blinded by the self-justifying rhetoric of his discourse. Indeed, one of the few truly personal comments he makes states explicitly that, like Shōtetsu in a later day,[22] he was disenchanted with a poetic world that was "divided into many currents, with cronies at poetic gatherings always ready with their various opinions, throwing my old heart into confusion and leaving me looking for the one path I first heard of long ago."[23]

When exasperated by the factionalism of his own day, Shōtetsu would look back to Teika as mentor. Tonna instead looked back to the latter's son, Tameie, whose works he characterized as "mellifluous and full of feeling."[24] Above all, what Tonna encouraged as the foundation for poetic art was the educated and disciplined sensibility, delicate and refined. His impatience with Kyōgoku Tamekane was less over the relative importance of "creativity" in composition than over the issue of whether poetic language should be elevated over ordinary language. One of his anecdotes makes the point somewhat obliquely:

> The late master Tameyo said: "Back in the days when Tameie was a captain in the Gate Guards, a Bishop something-or-other was always coming to him with questions about poetry. After hearing that in poetry 'One should put truth above all else, and be sure that you adhere to logic,' he came some days later and said, 'I have written a poem according to your instructions the other day. I wonder if I've got it right.'

> The peak of Fuji
>   appears to be everywhere
>   the exact same shape—

whether from that side over there
or from this side over here.

*fuji no yama / onaji sugata no / miyuru kana
anataomote mo / konataomote mo*

'This isn't what should result from putting logic above all
else,' Tameie said and broke out laughing."[25]

Perhaps it was the humor of this story that initially appealed
to Tonna. Nevertheless, there is a serious contention behind
it: that poetry should not be a mechanical business, not the
simple description in everyday language of nature observed
according to logic, or *kotowari*. Nor were ingenuity and clev-
erness enough, in his opinion, to sustain the enterprise. In-
stead, poetry for Tonna was a matter of deep thought and
feeling, and of the careful crafting of thought into elevated,
sonorous language—the sort of language that gains in power
by being read aloud at a poetry gathering. As Yoshimoto re-
ports it, Tonna's credo is actually straightforward: "What
Tonna always said was that one should put new meaning into
one's poems, delicately and with no exaggeration, stringing
the words together to beautiful effect."[26] That this was an
acceptable goal for many generations of Japanese poets in the
uta form is evidenced by Tonna's high reputation for nearly
five centuries after his death and by the enduring beauty of
his poems, which I hope is at least partially apparent in the
translations in this book.

In addition to translations of his *uta*—the thirty-one-
syllable classical form that was Tonna's primary genre—I
have also included a few examples of his *renga* links, which
are recorded in *Zoku Sōanshū*. A hint of the place of the new
genre in his practice is available in several of the anecdotes
recorded in *Seiashō*, including this one:

The late Master Tameyo said: "Tameie said, 'When I am
going to someone else's house for a poetry gathering, I pre-

pare one or two linked verse *hokku* [initiating verses]. . . .
Sometimes at the end of a gathering, suddenly someone
says, "Let's do some linked verse," and you don't want to
keep people waiting while you are coming up with a first
verse.' "27

If this indicates that linked verse was not taken as seriously
as composition in the *uta*, it is probably an accurate reflection
of the attitude of most court-poets in Tonna's day. It was only
later, and largely due to the efforts of Tonna's student and
friend Nijō Yoshimoto, that linked verse began to gain real
artistic credibility. Like most poets of his day, however, Tonna
seems to have composed linked verse quite often, usually, as
the anecdote indicates, after more formal *uta* gatherings. In
such settings, the atmosphere was often playful, with com-
position very much like a game, as in this couplet:

> Completely frozen over
>   and yet—still the waves rise.

> Moonlight resting
>   on the tips of pampas plumes
>   heavy with fall dew.28

> *kōredomo nao / nami wa tachikeri;*
> *tsuki yadoru / obana ga sue no / aki no tsuyu*

Here the two-line *maeku* (previous verse), whose author is
unknown, presents the poet with a riddle: How can waves
rise over frozen waters? Tonna answers in his three-line re-
sponse with an image of pampas grass (swaying like waves)
under a burden of dew in the moonlight—a properly courtly
response that would have been appreciated in the *za*.

   When Nijō Yoshimoto put together his famous an-
thology of linked verse, *Tsukubashū*, in 1356, eighteen of
Tonna's links (*tsukeku*) and one of his *hokku* were included—

more than twice the number accorded his teacher Tameyo, who was represented by only eight contributions. As the anecdote again intimates, masters of the *uta* were no doubt expected to take a leading role in linked verse as well, and Tonna was up to the task. While perhaps lacking the serious tone of the work of later poets such as Sōgi and Shinkei, his *renga* show a mastery of convention and the gentle beauty one grows used to in his *uta*:

> Yesterday, and then today
> the snow just keeps on falling.

> In pools, in rapids,
> the waters have frozen over—
> making not a sound.[29]

> *kinō mo kyō mo / yuki zo nao furu;*
> *fuchi mo se mo / kōreba mizu no / oto taete*

There is wordplay at work in this link, too, especially in the way the first line of the *tsukeku* mirrors the syntax of the *maeku*; but the final line moves beyond that, taking a step back from the scene that ends in the hushed silence of a snowfall that hides all to sound as well as sight. When Ichijō Kaneyoshi (1402–1481) later said that Tonna's *renga* were on a par with his *uta*,[30] perhaps he had such links in mind.

In every sense, Tonna was a master of the literary arts of his time. Through a lifetime of dedication to the art of composition, he achieved a level of artistry that made him the envy of all until the advent of new critical models, most of them adopted from the study of Western Romantic poetry, pushed his work to the margins. No student of Japanese poetry, however, can claim a full understanding of the native canon without some attention to this quintessential medieval master of the Way.

A NOTE ON THE TRANSLATIONS

In preparing the translations of the poems, I have used the texts of *Sōanshū* and *Zoku Sōanshū* published in volume 4 of [*Shinpen*] *Kokka taikan* (Tokyo: Kadokawa Shoten, 1986), both edited by Fukatsu Mutsuo. My interpretations have been aided by the short glosses of some individual poems provided by Inada Toshinori in his edition of *Tonna hōshi ei,* a selection of poems from *Sōanshū* that the poet made in 1357, which appears in volume 47 of *Shin nihon koten bungaku taikei* (Tokyo: Iwanami Shoten, 1990). Occasionally, I have also referred to the commentaries on *Sōanshū* and *Zoku Sōanshū* by the Edo scholar Motoori Norinaga (1730–1801) in volume 2 of *Motoori Norinaga zenshū* (Tokyo: Chikuma Shobō, 1968). In translating portions of *Seiashō,* I have used the text as published in volume 5 of *Nihon kagaku taikei* (Tokyo: Kazama Shobō, 1957) and also referred to Sasaki Takahiro et al., eds., *Karon kagaku shūsei,* volume 10 (Tokyo: Miyai Shoten, 1999).

Readers wanting an explanation of the format used in my translations of Tonna's poems may refer to my comments at the end of the introduction to an earlier book, *Unforgotten Dreams: Poems by the Zen Monk Shōtetsu.* In brief, I have adopted an approach that I hope helps reflect the syntax and image-order of the originals. Each of the five lines that make up a complete *uta* are thus "anchored" on the left margin, with the syntactic patterns of the originals then represented by "jogging" of lines to the right, suggesting the way the Japanese poems seem to "unfold." I have also tried wherever possible to stick to the 5–7–5–7–7 syllable format of the originals, which I find useful as a form to work against in order to create rhythm and tension.

NOTES

1. *Shirin shūha,* in *Nihon kagaku taikei,* vol. 6 (Tokyo: Kazama Shobō, 1956), p. 375.

2. Inada Toshinori, *Waka shitennō no Kenkyū* (Tokyo: Kasama Shoin, 1999), pp. 41–42.

3. *Kinrai fūteishō,* in *Nihon kagaku taikei,* vol. 5 (Tokyo: Kazama Shobō, 1957), p. 141.

4. *Sōanshū* 1208. Poem 78 in this volume.

5. Steven D. Carter, "Mixing Memories: Linked Verse and the Fragmentation of the Past," *Harvard Journal of Asiatic Studies* 48 (1988): 6.

6. Inada argues that *Tonna hōshi ei* was probably submitted to the Poetry Bureau at the time *Shin senzaishū* was being compiled, *Sōanshū* being put together shortly thereafter (*Waka shitennō no Kenkyū,* pp. 53–56).

7. Inoue Muneo, *Chūsei kadanshi no kenkyū, Muromachi zenki* (Tokyo: Kazama Shobō, 1961), p. 49.

8. Ibid.

9. *Rakusho roken,* in *Nihon kagaku taikei,* vol. 5 (Tokyo: Kazama Shobō, 1957), p. 191.

10. *Zoku Sōanshū* 65. Poem 96 in this volume.

11. *Shin kokinshū* 67. See note to poem 96 in this volume.

12. Robert H. Brower and Steven D. Carter, *Conversations with Shōtetsu* (Ann Arbor: Center for Japanese Studies, University of Michigan, 1992), pp. 105–106.

13. *Sōanshū* 204. Poem 13 in this volume.

14. *Sōanshū* 7. Poem 1 in this volume.

15. *Sōanshū* 86. Poem 4 in this volume.

16. *Kinrai fūteishō,* p. 141.

17. *Sōanshū* 741. Poem 35 in this volume.

18. Imagawa Ryōshun was probably the first to utter this exaggeration, in *Nigonshō,* in *Nihon kagaku taikei,* vol. 5 (Tokyo: Kazama Shobō, 1957), p. 173.

19. *Sōanshū* 655. Poem 27 in this volume.

20. *Zoku Sōanshū* 315. Poem 120 in this volume.

21. Steven D. Carter, "Seeking What the Masters Sought: Masters, Disciples, and Poetic Enlightenment in Medieval Japan," in Robert Borgen, Thomas Hare, and Sharalyn Orbaugh, eds., *The Distant Isle: Studies and Translations of Japanese Literature in Honor of Robert H. Brower* (Ann Arbor:

Center for Japanese Studies, University of Michigan, 1996), p. 52.

22. Brower and Carter, *Conversations with Shōtetsu,* pp. 33–37.

23. See p. 212.

24. See p. 212.

25. See pp. 189–190.

26. *Kinrai fūteishō,* p. 143. J. *atarashiki kokoro o yasuraki ni koto-gotoshiku nakute utsukushiku tsusuku beshi.*

27. See p. 196.

28. *Zoku Sōanshū* 584. Poem 140 in this volume.

29. *Zoku Sōanshū* 564. Poem 135 in this volume.

30. Steven D. Carter, *Regent Redux: A Life of the Statesman-Scholar Ichijō Kaneyoshi* (Ann Arbor: Center for Japanese Studies, University of Michigan, 1996), p. 238.

THE POEMS

ON "EARLY SPRING," FROM THREE POEMS COMPOSED AT THE POETRY BUREAU

In fair Yoshino
the wind low
            on the mountain slopes
grows more chilly still;
and half-hidden
            in the haze—
fine flakes of falling snow.

*miyoshino no / yama no shitakaze / nao saete
kasumigakure ni / awayuki zo furu*

2

"PLUM BLOSSOMS BEFORE THE MOON"

Leaving unclosed
my door
     of black pine,
          I go
to bed for the night,
pillowed on an arm
         awash
in plum scent—and light
          from the moon.*

*maki no to o / sasade nuru yo no / tamakura ni
ume ga ka nagara / tsuki zo utsureru*

---

*An allusive variation on *Kokinshū* 690, an anonymous poem: Will
you come to me / or I to you? I wonder / with the hesitant moon,
/ and leave unclosed my pine door / to keep watch from my bed
(kimi ya komu / ware ya yukamu no / isayoi ni / maki no itado
mo / sasazu nenikeri).

3

[ON "WILLOWS"] FROM AMONG THREE
POEMS COMPOSED AT THE HOME OF THE
NIJŌ LAY-MONK MAJOR COUNSELOR
[TAMEYO]

All atangle
in the wind,
        but then slowly
after its passing
disentangling on their own—
threads
        on the green willows.

*fukimidasu / kaze no ato yori / yagate mata
kokoro to tokuru / aoyagi no ito*

4

"RETURNING GEESE"

Even in
      a world
full of false promises
they will not
          forget
their pledge
         to come back home—
those geese now flying away.*

itsuwari no / aru yo ni dani mo / furusato no
chigiri wasurezu / kari no yukuran

---

*Wild geese fly back to the continent each spring, after spending the winter in Japan.

"RETURNING GEESE, IN THE HAZE"

Gazing far, I see
haze spreading
                    into the distance;
but in the gaps,
appearing here
                    and then there—
wild geese
          in one tattered line.

nagamureba / kasumihatete wa / taedae ni
mata arawaruru / kari no hitotsura

6

"BLOSSOMS AT NIGHT"

On a night in spring
the moon
        has not emerged yet
above the branches—
where
        on the mountain rim
blossoms are first
                to appear.*

*haru no yo no / tsuki wa konoma o / ideyarade
mazu yama no ha no / hana zo mieyuku*

---

*An allusive variation on *Shin gosenshū* 323, by Kamo no Ujihisa:
On the mountain rim / not yet emerging is the moon / so much
awaited; / first to rise into the clear / is the call of a stag (yama no
ha ni / mataruru tsuki wa / ideyarade / mazu suminoboru / saoshika
no koe).

ON "BLOSSOMS AT DAWN," FROM THREE POEMS COMMISSIONED BY THE UTSUNOMIYA TŌTOMI LAY-MONK RENCHI

It was the dawn
        moon
I had been waiting up for—
when in its light
appeared
        the first glimpses
of cherry blossoms
        on the hills.

machiizuru / ariake no tsuki no / kagenagara
arawaresomuru / yamazakura kana

8

"BLOSSOMS AT AN ANCIENT CAPITAL"

If those many springs
there had been
          no blossoms there
to attract men's eyes,
then how much more
          a ruin
would be
      the capital at Shiga.*

*haru o hete / hana ni hitome no / nokorazu wa
shiga no furusato / nao ya arenan*

---

*Shiga, located near the southern tip of Lake Biwa, had been the site of the capital in the seventh century.

ON "THINKING OF BLOSSOMS AT NIGHT,"
COMPOSED WHEN THE CHAMBERLAIN-
MIDDLE COUNSELOR [TAMEAKIRA] INVITED
PEOPLE FROM THE POETRY BUREAU TO GO
SEE THE BLOSSOMS

On into the night
it comes
         right along with me:
that same image
—seen until
            the sun went down—
of blossoms
         in the branches.

yoru wa nao / waga mi ni zo sou / kururu made
kozue ni mitsuru / hana no omokage

10

Here in my cottage
I forget
     my loneliness,
thanks to the blossoms—
only to find myself waiting
for someone
       to show them to.*

sabishisa wa / hana ni wasururu / yado naredo
miseba ya to nomi / hito zo mataruru

---

*An echo of *Shin chokusenshū* 1049, by Minamoto no Mitsuyuki:
Beneath the trees / I forget my forlorn state, / thanks to the blossoms— / though after spring is over / no consolation remains (mi no usa o / hana ni wasururu / ko no moto wa / haru yori nochi no / nagusame zo naki).

ON "BREAKING OFF A BRANCH," FROM A
TEN-POEM CONTEST AT THE HOME OF THE
MINAMOTO MAJOR COUNSELOR
[CHIKAFUSA]

If only words
had the power
                    to describe
the cherry blossoms—
then one would need
                    no broken branch
to tell people
            of their color.*

koto no ha mo / oyobu bakari no / iro naraba
orade ya hana o / hito ni kataran

---

*An allusive variation on *Kokinshū* 55, by Sosei (written on seeing
cherry blossoms in the mountains): Just looking at them / how can
one tell anyone / about the cherry blossoms? / Let us each break
off a sprig / to take home as a gift! (mite nomi ya / hito ni kataramu
/ sakurabana / tegoto ni orite / iezuto ni semu).

"FALLEN BLOSSOMS IN THE RIVER,"
COMPOSED AT THE HOME OF
MINAMOTO NO MUNEUJI

Yoshino River:
where on the peaks
                    cherry blossoms
must now be falling—
to make on unfrozen
                    waters
a layer
        of white snow.

yoshinokawa / takane no sakura / chirinu rashi
kōranu mizu ni / tsumoru shirayuki

"FALLING BLOSSOMS"

Not at all
        like snow,
so ready to melt away—
these cherry blossoms:
fallen but then
           lifted again
by storm winds
           in the garden.

kiegate no / yuki to mo miezu / sakurabana
tsumoreba harau / niwa no arashi ni

14

Yes, it was the rain
that sent
      the cherry blossoms
into their decline,
but on the ground
           in the garden
they pile up
      as snow.

*ame ni koso / shiorehatsu tomo / sakurabana
niwa wa yuki to ya / furitsumoruran*

15

WRITTEN AS A BLOSSOM POEM AT THE
HOME OF TOSHIZANE, GOVERNOR GENERAL
OF DAZAIFU

None
        seemed to be left
among the green leaves,
                        I thought—
but then from among
the branches,
            a trickle still
of descending
            cherry blossoms.

nokoru to mo / mienu aoba no / kozue yori
ima mo taedae / chiru sakura kana

16

In the depths of night,
I wonder, "Could it
            really be—
a cuckoo's call?"
—heard from far back in the hills
for the first time
            this year.

sayo fukete / sore ka to bakari / hototogisu
miyamanagara no / hatsune zo kiku

"CUCKOO AT LAKESIDE"

Into the Sea of Grebes*
we row out and stop
              to listen—
to a cuckoo
calling now,
           in the distance,
off at the mountain's base.

niho no umi ni / kogiidete kikeba / hototogisu
yamamoto tōku / ima zo naku naru

---

*An epithet for Lake Biwa.

18

"RICE SPROUTS," FROM A SEVENTY-POEM
SEQUENCE COMPOSED AT THE HOME OF
THE TŌJI'IN POSTHUMOUS MINISTER OF
THE LEFT [TAKAUJI]

The rain
     clears away
and the evening sun
         shines down—
on paddy workers
who rest now
     from pulling sprouts
to dry skirts
     drenched in the fields.

*ame harete / yūhi sasu nari / sanae toru
tago no mosuso ya / nurete hosuran*

"ORANGE BLOSSOMS AT A HUT IN THE NIGHT"

Nearby my bed,
flowering orange
         fills
the night
         with its scent—
until both dream
         and reality
take me into the past.*

*neya chikaku / hanatachibana no / niou yo wa
yume mo utsutsu mo / mukashi narikeri*

---

*An allusion to *Kokinshū* 139, an anonymous poem: Catching the
scent / of orange trees that wait to bloom / until the Fifth Month,
/ I recall from long ago / the scented sleeves of one now gone
(satsuki matsu / hanatachibana no / ka o kageba / mukashi no hito
no / sode no ka zo suru).

20

FROM A SOLO HUNDRED-VERSE SEQUENCE

After fretting so
over how little time
                    remained
before break of day
one resents
            even the emergence
of the moon
            on a summer night.

akeyasuki / nagori o kanete / omou ni wa
izuru mo oshiki / natsu no yo no tsuki

"THE COOL OF A SUMMER EVENING," FROM A POEM CONTEST HELD BY SAISHŌ TENJI

Even the voices
of cicadas
        are silenced;
after close of day,
still there
        in the branches
is the wind—
        blowing, ah, so cool.

naku semi no / koe mo kikoezu / kurehatete
kozue ni nokoru / kaze zo suzushiki

"DEW ON THE FIELDS," COMPOSED AT THE
HOME OF NAGAHIDE, GOVERNOR OF HYŌGO

Blown every which way:
dewdrops
      forming
           but to scatter,
white jewels
      glistening
all across the Yoko Moors
in the first wind
      of autumn.

*fukinikeri / okeba katsu chiru / shiratsuyu no
tama no yokono no / aki no hatsukaze*

23

ON "LINGERING HEAT," FOR A TEN-POEM
SEQUENCE [AT THE HOUSE OF THE
MIKOHIDARI MAJOR COUNSELOR]

Autumn has come,
yet still I must use
                    a fan
to stir the air.
This year
          the season will begin
with dewfall
               first of all.

aki kite mo / ōgi no kaze o / narasu kana
kotoshi wa tsuyu ya / saki ni okuran

24

ON "BUSH CLOVER," WRITTEN FOR A THOUSAND-VERSE SEQUENCE

Nowadays
        not a friend
whose heart
        goes back to the past
is left in the world.
But on a branch
        grown old like me—
blossoms on autumn bush clover.*

*ima wa yo ni / moto no kokoro no / tomo mo nashi
oite furue no / akihagi no hana*

---

*An allusive variation on *Kokinshū* 219, by Ōshikōchi no Mitsune (written after he chatted with someone he had known long before, when they met out in the autumn fields): Seeing these blossoms / upon the aging branches / of autumn bush clover, / I know that those old feelings / have not yet been forgotten (akihagi no / furue ni sakeru / hana mireba / moto no kokoro wa / wasurezariheri).

25

Making known
the boundlessness
    of the sky—
the peak of Fuji,
where above the smoke
      appear
the bright rays
    of the moon.

kagiri naki / sora mo shirarete / fuji no ne no
kemuri no ue ni / izuru tsukikage

26

ON "THE MOON BETWEEN BAMBOOS,"
FROM A FIFTY-POEM SEQUENCE AT THE
HOME OF THE SHŌGO'IN PRINCE OF THE
SECOND RANK [KAKUJO]

Down through
            fine branches
spills the light of the moon,
casting the shadows
of bamboo leaves
            on the window
even in the dark
            of midnight.

saeda yori / tsuki wa morikite / take no ha no
kage sae mado ni / utsuru yowa kana

ON "THE LATE AUTUMN MOON,"
WHEN HE COMPOSED POEMS AT THE
COTTAGE OF KENKŌ

Through gaps in the clouds
that drop showers
          as they pass,
moonlight
     spills down—
fading quickly
       into the dark
of the dusky autumn sky.

*shigure suru / kumo no taema o / moru tsuki no
hayaku mo kururu / aki no sora kana*

ON "NIGHT SHOWERS," WRITTEN AT THE
HOME OF YORIYASU, MASTER OF THE
PALACE TABLE OFFICE

Even the showers
fall,
     then stop,
          then fall again
in brief bursts of sound—
as I lie awake
        in the night,
worried
     by the world's restless ways.

shigure sae / furimi furazumi / oto sunari
sadamenaki yo o / omou nezame ni

"ROOFTOP SHOWERS"

On a winter
            night
gaps
        in my bedchamber eaves
show no hint of dawn;
over and over again
the showers come
                falling down.*

*fuyu no yo no / neya no itama wa / akeyarade
ikudo to naku / furu shigure kana*

---

*An allusive variation on *Senzaishū* 766, by Shun'e: All through
the night / I am so lost in longing / that even the gaps / in my
bedchamber eaves, I hate / for showing no hint of dawn (yomo-
sugara / mono omou koro wa / akeyaranu / neya no hima sae /
tsurenakarikeri).

"FALLEN LEAVES ON A PATH"

Under evergreens
I walk
      along a pathway
now gone to sight
beneath autumn leaves
              strewn there
by winter's mountain winds.

tokiwagi no / kage fumu michi mo / mienu made
momiji fukishiku / fuyu no yamakaze

FOR A SCREEN AT KANGAKU'IN DEPICTING
WINTER AT YASUKAWA

At Moru Mountain
there must be
                no leaves left
even low on the trees—
so muted
            is the sound
of waves on Yasu River.*

*moruyama no / shitaba nokorazu / narinu rashi
yasunokawanami / oto musebu nari*

---

*An allusive variation on *Kokinshū* 260, by Ki no Tsurayuki: At
Moru Mountain / white dewdrops and constant showers / have
trickled down so / that even the lowest leaves / are dyed now in
autumn hues (shiratsuyu mo / shigure mo itaku / moruyama wa/
shitaba nokorazu / irozukinikeri).

32

"WINTER MOON"

The moon remains,
its shining
           now unobscured
by leaves on the trees—
gone
      in a storm
                that has left
nothing
      of autumn behind.*

*tsuki zo nao / konoha kumorade / nokorikeru
aki no katami wa / tomenu arashi ni*

---

*An allusive variation on *Shin kokinshū* 593, by Gishūmon'in no
Tango: After the rough winds / of a storm have passed and gone,
/ above the high peak / appears the moon, unobscured / by leaves
on the trees (fukiharau / arashi no nochi no / takane yori / konoha
kumorade / tsuki ya izuramu).

33

"WINTER MOON," FOR THREE POEMS
COMPOSED AT THE MONTHLY POETRY
MEETING OF DHARMA SIGN JŌBEN

As the hour grows late,
the sound
        of the storm
                in the sky
rings out,
        cold and clear;
in gaps between the clouds—
frozen rays
        of moonlight.

fukeyukeba / sora ni arashi no / oto saete
kumoma ni kōru / tsuki no kage kana

ON "WATER BIRDS," FROM THREE POEMS
COMMISSIONED BY THE OGURA
CONSULTANT-MIDDLE CAPTAIN [SANENA]

The shallows along shore
must by now
            be frozen over:
for out in the pools
of the mountain river—
                        the calls
of frolicking
            water birds.

asaki se wa / kōri ya suran / yamakawa no
fuchi ni zo sawagu / mizutori no koe

35

WRITTEN WHEN SOME WATERFOWL
RAISED BY CHILDREN WERE RELEASED
INTO THE WATERS OF HIROSAWA POND
["BROAD POND"]

Accustomed by now
to life
     in the rocky narrows
of a garden stream,
broad, indeed,
          to the ducks
               must seem
the waters of Broad Pond.

yarimizu no / sebaki iwama ni / suminarete
sazo hirosawa no / ike no oshidori

"HAIL ON DWARF BAMBOO," FROM A POEM CONTEST AT KONRENJI

Enough
      to brush off
the evening dew
          on the leaves
of the dwarf bamboo
set astir
      by its clatter—
just that much hail
          comes down.

oto sayagu / ozasa ga ue no / yūshimo o
harau bakari ni / furu arare kana

"HAIL AT AN OLD HOUSE," AT THE HOME
OF THE FORMER TŌ MAJOR COUNSELOR
[TAMEYO]

So frost-withered
is the Secret Grass*
                that grows
out beneath the eaves
that it cannot even
                conceal
the sound
        of falling hail.

*nokiba naru / shinobu no kusa wa / shimogarete
oto mo kakurezu / furu arare kana*

Shinobugusa, a variety of fern. The verb *shinobu* means "to yearn
for in secret."

38

ON "SNOW ON CEDARS," FROM
FIFTY POEMS AT SHŌGO'IN

Has the new day dawned?
A grove of cedars*
                        begins
to rise into view;
from snow
                on the mountain peak,
a cloud goes
                        breaking away.

*akenuru ka / sugi no muradachi / miesomete
onoe no yuki ni / kumo zo wakaruru*

Sugi, technically cryptomeria.

"SNOW ON A BARRIER ROAD"

At Meeting Hill
people coming,
               people going,
leave marks
           clear to see:
yet still
          too hard to follow
for this morning's
              snow.*

*ausaka ya / yuku mo kaeru mo / ato miete
sekiji tadoranu / kesa no shirayuki*

---

*An allusive variation on *Gosenshū* 1089, by Semimaru: Here it is:
the gate / where people coming and going / must part company, /
where both friends and strangers meet— / on the slopes of Meeting
Hill (kore ya kono / yuku mo kaeru mo / wakarete wa / shiru mo
shiranu mo / ausaka no seki).

"SNOW ON THE BAY"

Even the pathways
of fisherfolk
       working along shore
are covered over;
and on boats
       plying the bay—
white snow piling up.

amabito no / isobe no michi mo / uzumorete
ura kogu fune ni / tsumoru shirayuki

41

"SNOW DEEP IN THE MOUNTAINS,"
WRITTEN AT THE HOME OF THE NIJŌ
MAJOR COUNSELOR [TAMEYO]

Pile up, then, snow
falling
          on the mountain peak
where I have come
to escape
          the cruel world—
block all paths
          to my return!

*tsumore tada / irinishi yama no / mine no yuki
ukiyo ni kaeru / michi mo naki made*

42

As swiftly
        as clouds
traveling the mountain crests
on the winds
        of a storm—
so swiftly
        do I follow
the one
        who has swept me away.

arashi fuku / yama no onoe o / yuku kumo no
hayaku mo hito o / kakete koitsutsu

ON "LOVE, RELATED TO 'CLOUD,'" FROM
FIVE POEMS COMPOSED FOR THE MONTHLY
POETRY MEETING OF NAGAHIDE

High on the peak
of cloud-capped
                    Mount Fuji
the smoke is rising*—
and no more
                    easy to hide
is the burning
                    in my heart.

kumo kakaru / fuji no takane ni / tatsu kemuri
kakurehatsu beki / mi no omoi ka wa

---

*Mount Fuji was an active volcano as late as the early eighteenth
century.

ON "LOVE KEPT SECRET FOR A LONG TIME,"
FROM A TEN-POEM SEQUENCE AT THE
HOME OF THE FORMER TŌ MAJOR
COUNSELOR [TAMEYO]

Through so many years
did I suffer
              the agony
of keeping our secret—
that even now
              I cannot bear
to let the truth be known.

*toshi o hete / shinobishi kata no / kurushisa o
omou ni sae zo / morashikanenuru*

45

The heart
　　　　of someone
who refuses to respond—
what
　　　　to compare it to?
The rocks and the trees
　　　　　　　　after all,
do not bear a man
　　　　　　　ill will.*

*tsuremonaki / kokoro o nani ni / tatoemashi
iwaki wa hito o / itoi ya wa suru*

---

*An allusive variation on *Senzaishū* 758, by Kamo no Masahira: So
hard it is / for me to get to meet her / that almost I think / the
heart of she who spurns me / must be a rock or a tree (au koto no
/ kaku katakereba / tsuremonaki / hito no kokoro ya / iwaki na-
ruramu).

46

"LOVING IN SECRET, UNABLE TO MEET"

My very life
I would give
        in pursuit
of the one I love.
Why then
        do I begrudge
the ruin
        of my good name?

koishinamu / inochi o dani mo / nagekanu ni
ukina bakari o / nani oshimuran

"LOVE, RELATED TO 'SMOKE,'" FROM A
HUNDRED-POEM SEQUENCE AT THE HOME
OF THE MINISTER OF POPULAR AFFAIRS
[TAMEFUJI]

Though I die
            for love
I will not
            bewail my fate—
if only in turn
she will think fondly
                  of me
as one gone to smoke
                  for her.*

*koishinan / mi o ba nagekaji / ware yue no
keburi ni nashite / aware to mo miba*

---

*An echo of *Senzaishū* 774, by Fujiwara no Sanekuni (sent to a
woman): Should I die for love, / please at least remember / that it
was for you. / —even if that cruel heart of yours / is still cold
toward me now (koishinaba / ware yue to dani / omoiideyo / sakoso
wa tsuraki / kokoro nari tomo).

48

ON "LOVE—GROWN ACCUSTOMED TO,"
FROM A FIVE-POEM SEQUENCE AT THE
HOME OF THE MINISTER OF POPULAR
AFFAIRS [TAMEFUJI]

Those no longer
at a distance
      from each other
suffer all the more,
when every slight,
      every pain—
not a thing remains
      hidden.

utokaranu / naka zo itodo / kurushikere
uki mo tsuraki mo / kakure nakereba

"UNREQUITED LOVE," FOR A FIVE-POEM
SEQUENCE AT THE HOME OF SHŌGO'IN
[KAKUJO]

Should I die of love,
even then
            I would continue
to feel rejected—
knowing how halfheartedly
she would say,
            "Ah, what a shame."

*koishinan / nochi sae tsurashi / naozari ni
aware to iwamu / hito no kokoro wa*

50

ON "LOVE ON A MOONLIT NIGHT," FROM A
TEN-POEM SEQUENCE COMPOSED AT THE
HOME OF THE TŌ MAJOR COUNSELOR
[TAMEYO]

Such a waste of time!
Gazing up
        at the moon
night after night,
thinking
        she too will see it—
and feel the same
            in her heart.*

*hakanashi ya / tsuki miru hodo no / yoru yoru ni
kayou kokoro o / tanomu bakari wa*

---

*An allusive variation on *Shūishū* 787, by Minamoto no Saneakira
(sent to a woman on a night when the moon was shining bright):
Perhaps in your heart / you do not feel for me / the love I feel for
you; / but the moon on this night— / Surely you must see it, too?
(koishisa wa / onaji kokoro ni / arazu tomo / koyoi no tsuki o /
mizarame ya).

"LOVE IN THE MIST," FROM TEN POEMS
COMPOSED AT THE HOME OF THE MINISTER
OF POPULAR AFFAIRS [TAMEFUJI]

I gaze out,
            but still
the sky is empty
                of all
but the autumn mist—
as aimless
            as my passion,
with no place to go.*

*nagamete mo / munashiki sora no / akigiri ni
itodo omoi no / yuku kata mo nashi*

---

*An allusive variation on *Kokinshū* 488, an anonymous poem: The love I feel / seems to fill the very void / of the empty sky. / For the thoughts I send out / have no where else to go (*waga koi wa / munashiki sora ni / michinu rashi / omoiyaredomo / yuku kata mo nashi*).

ON "LOVE IN WINTER," FROM WHEN WE
COMPOSED POEMS AT THE HOUSE OF
DHARMA SIGN JŌBEN

My tears
          of longing
must share something in common
with the sky above:
for off there
               in the distance
a cloud, too,
                    begins to shower.*

omoiyaru / namida ya sora ni / taguuran
sonata no kumo mo / shigurete zo yuku

---

*An allusive variation on *Shin kokinshū* 1107, by Fujiwara no
Shunzei (sent to a woman on a rainy day): Overwrought with love,
/ I gazed out upon the sky / above where you dwell— / and saw
the haze parted there / by a shower of spring rain (omou amari /
sonata no sora o / nagamureba / kasumi o wakete / harusame zo
furu).

53

ON "WAITING FOR LOVE ON AN AUTUMN
EVENING," FOR A FIFTEEN-POEM SEQUENCE
ON THE NIGHT OF THE FIFTEENTH DAY OF
THE EIGHTH MONTH, AT THE HOME OF THE
MINISTER OF POPULAR AFFAIRS [TAMEFUJI]

The sun
  in autumn
swiftly gives way
    to darkness,
but to no avail—
at least not for one
    who waits
a man
  who will not hurry.

aki no hi no / hodo naku kururu / kai mo nashi
hito no isoganu / naka no chigiri wa

ON "WAITING FOR LOVE IN SECRET,"
WRITTEN FOR A FIVE-POEM SEQUENCE
AT THE HOME OF THE MIKOHIDARI MAJOR
COUNSELOR [TAMESADA]

Wait a moment
                    there
on the rim
            of the mountain,
you moon at midnight!
If you come out now,
                        I will be
bereft
        of explanations.*

*yama no ha ni / shibashi matareyo / yowa no tsuki
idenaba iwamu / koto no ha mo nashi*

---

*An allusive variation on *Shūishū* 782, by Hitomaro (topic un-
known): That I was waiting / for the moon to emerge / from foot-
wearying hills— / that's what I told people, / while really I waited
for you (ashihiki no / yama yori izuru / tsuki matsu to / hito ni
wa iite / kimi o koso mate).

"LOVE, RELATED TO 'RAIN'"

To expect him
to be undeterred
               by rain—
that would be too much;
but, ah, to be certain,
                  at least,
of the breaks
          between showers!

furu ame ni / sawaranu made wa / kataku to mo
harema o tanomu / chigiri to mogana

ON "WAITING FOR LOVE, NIGHT AFTER
NIGHT," FOR A FIVE-POEM SEQUENCE AT
THE HOME OF THE MIKOHIDARI MAJOR
COUNSELOR [TAMESADA]

A single night,
that is all
       one needs to know
it was a lie;
what am I hoping for,
          then,
to persevere
      in waiting?

*hitoyo ni mo / uki itsuwari wa / shiraruru ni
nani no tanomi ni / taete matsuran*

57

"LOVE—WAITING BENEATH THE SKY"

Forlorn, I wait
'til this night too
                ends with dawn.
How could I have thought
that the sound
            of a cockcrow
pains
      only those who must part?

machiwabite / koyoi mo akenu / tori no ne no
uki o wakare to / nani omoiken

58

Though it drifts
               my way,
can I really be so sure?
A cloud blown
               by winds
as it travels
               through the sky
is in the end a fickle thing.

*nabiku tomo / e ya wa tanomamu / fuku kaze ni
sora yuku kumo no / utsuriyasusa o*

59

We heard the call—
but still
      we put off parting;
until
      —before we heard
the cock calling once again—
night have given way
             to dawn.

nakinuredo / wakare mo yarade / tori no ne no
kikoenu made ni / akuru yowa kana

60

"PARTING BENEATH THE MOON,"
WRITTEN WHEN WE WERE COMPOSING
POEMS AT FUDANKŌJI

Will I ever
see it
    just this way
        again?
On sleeves of white hemp
now parting
        from each other—
light
    from the moon at dawn.*

*kono mama ni / mata ya mizaran / shirotae no
sode no wakare no / ariake no tsuki*

---

*An allusive variation on *Shin kokinshū* 1336, by Fujiwara no Teika
(from *The Minase Fifteen Poem Contest*): When we parted / dew-
drops fell down on my sleeves / of pure white hemp— / your
coldness as harsh as the hue / of the piercing autumn wind (shirotae
no sode no wakare ni / tsuyu ochite / mi ni shimu iro no / akikaze
zo fuku). Also probably an echo of *Shin kokinshū* 114, by Fujiwara
no Shunzei (written for a five-poem sequence at the house of the
Regent-Chancellor): Will I see this again? / A hunt for cherry blos-
soms / on Katano Moor— / petals of snow scattering / in the first
faint light of dawn (mata ya mimu / katano no mino no / sakuragari
/ hana no yuki chiru / haru no akebono).

"LOVE—THE MORNING AFTER," WRITTEN AT
THE HOME OF THE LAY-MONK FORMER
CHANCELLOR [KINKATA]

When we parted,
he promised
       nothing—not even
"Wait 'til this evening."
Yet as soon
     as I fall asleep
I see him
    in my dreams.

kure o dani / mate to mo hito wa / chigiranedo
yagate matane no / yume ni miru kana

62

"LOVE, RELATED TO 'MOON'"

His receding
　　　　image
is all that remains
　　　　　　to me,
clear in my mind—
as the moon
　　　　behind teardrops
is unblurred
　　　　not a single night.

wasuraruru / omokage bakari / sadaka nite
tsuki wa namida ni / haruru yo mo nashi

ON "LOVE, RELATED TO 'MOON,'" FOR A
TEN-POEM SEQUENCE ON THE MOON FOR
THE AKAI PRINCE

So feckless a hope—
that the moon
            crossing the sky
would be enough
to keep us
            in the same world—
held together
            by a memory.*

*ada nari ya / sora yuku tsuki o / katami nite
nao onaji yo to / tanomu bakari wa*

---

*An allusive variation on *Shūishū* 470, an anonymous poem (when
Tachibana no Tadamoto was secretly visiting a certain man's daugh-
ter, he was transferred to a distant place and sent this to her): Don't
forget me— / though I go as far away / as the clouds above. / Not
'til the moon crossing the sky / comes around this way again (was-
uru na yo / hodo wa kumoi ni / narinu to mo / sora yuku tsuki
no / meguriau made). The poem also appears in section 11 of *Ise
monogatari*.

64

ON "MEETING AGAIN, AFTER LOVE HAD
ENDED," WRITTEN WHEN POEMS WERE
BEING COMPOSED AT SŌRINJI, UPON A
VISIT FROM THE REIZEI MAJOR COUNSELOR
[TAMEUJI]

It makes no sense!
—to get entangled
                    again
after so much time!
In the air,
            the dangling end
of a broken
            spider's thread.

imasara ni / kuru mo hakanaki / chigiri kana
sora ni taenishi / sasagani no ito

"LOVE, RELATED TO 'FLOWER,'"
WRITTEN FOR A POEM CONTEST HELD BY
SAISHŌ TENJI

The wilting flower
in the heart
        of one whose love
has died and gone
in the end fades
        utterly—
down to its very hue.*

*utsuriyuku / kokoro no hana no / hate wa mata
iro miyuru made / narinikeru kana*

---

*An allusive variation on *Kokinshū* 797, by Ono no Komachi (topic unknown): What is it that fades / without a change in color? / It is the flower / in the heart of those who love / in this world of ours (iro miede / utsurou mono wa / yo no naka no / hito no kokoro no / hana ni zo arikeru).

"DISTANT LOVE," WRITTEN AT THE HOME OF
THE MIKOHIDARI MAJOR COUNSELOR
[TAMESADA]

If even in dreams
we cannot meet,
        then how am I
to send a message?
Here on this Gloomy
        Mountain road
I meet no one at all.*

*yume ni dani / miezu to ikade / tsuge yaran
utsunoyamaji wa / au hito mo nashi*

---

*An allusive variation on *Shin kokinshū* 904, an anonymous poem
(sent back to the capital with someone he met at Utsuyama in
Suruga): In Suruga, / around Gloomy Mountain, / neither while
awake / nor yet again in my dreams / do I meet a soul (suruga
naru / utsu no yamabe no / utsutsu ni mo / yume ni mo hito ni /
awanu narikeri). The poem also appears in section 9 of *Ise mono-
gatari.*

"THE END OF LOVE," WRITTEN AT THE
HOME OF THE MINAMOTO MIDDLE
COUNSELOR [TOMOYUKI]

The years
       passed by
and I had thought that
           at last
I could rest secure.
Why now,
     then,
         after all this time,
does he seem to drift away?

toshi mo henu / sasuga ima wa to / tanomaruru
nochi shi mo hito no / tōzakaruran

68

"DAWN LOVE," WRITTEN WHEN FUJIWARA
MOTOTŌ WAS COMPOSING POEMS FOR THE
NEW HIE SHRINE

As the sky brightens,
in gaps
        between the clouds—stars,
shining faintly through,
as few in number
              as visits
from the one
       who pledged his love.

akewataru / kumoma no hoshi no / sanomi nado
mare ni nariyuku / chigiri naruran

FROM A SOLO HUNDRED-POEM SEQUENCE

But surely, no—
you cannot
      have forgotten!
Was it someone else
who long ago
      vowed his love
with promises,
        night after night?

sasuga yomo / wasureji mono o / inishie mo
hito ya wa iishi / yoyo no kanegoto

ON "LOVE CONCEALED AFTER A PLEDGE,"
FROM A FIVE-POEM SEQUENCE AT THE
HOME OF THE CAPTAIN OF THE LEFT
GUARDS [TADAYOSHI]

We pledged our love,
but all
     to no avail—
since I do not know
where
     in those far, cloudy hills
the pheasant has flown.

*chigirishi mo / kai koso nakere / kumo no iru
tōyamadori no / yukue shiraneba*

7

"LOVE AT AN END"

Now, at last,
        I know:
that when
        I waited to see him
night after night,
beneath it all
        already
in his heart
        he had changed.

*ima zo shiru / machimishi koro no / yona yona mo
shita ni wa kawaru / kokoro narikeri*

"BROKEN PLEDGE OF LOVE"

Nothing comes
              from him,
not so much as a note
                    asking,
"Do you remember
the pledge of love
              we made?"—
so distant has he become.

chigirishi wa / omoiizu ya to / tou hodo no
tayori dani naku / tōzakaritsutsu

73

"LOVE AT AN END"

The pledge
        we exchanged
in a dream-world
          long ago
has never changed;
what turned out
        to be fickle
is the world
      of reality.

mukashi ni mo / kawaranu yume no / chigiri kana
hakanaki mono wa / utsutsu narikeri

AT NACHI WATERFALL IN KUMANO

So high is the peak
that the waterfall
    descends
from out of the clouds—
making a shower of rain
that clears
   never for a day.

*yama fukami / kumo yori otsuru / takitsuse no
atari no ame wa / haruru hi mo nashi*

WRITTEN IN THE AUTUMN, WHEN HE FIRST
MOVED TO HIS COTTAGE AT NINNAJI

I took up
      life here
in this village in the hills
in the moon
        season;
and before long
          my heart, too,
had decided it would stay.*

*yamazato ni / tsuki no koro shimo / sumisomete
yagate kokoro no / tomarinuru kana*

---

*An allusive variation on *Goshūishū* 345, by Fujiwara no Kanefusa
(describing a scene on a standing screen in which someone was
standing next to a carriage, looking at the autumn leaves): It's still
a long way / until we reach our home / back in the mountains; /
yet my heart wants to stay / here amid the autumn leaves (furusato
wa / mada tōkeredomo / momijiba no / iro ni kokoro no / to-
marinuru kana).

ON "MOUNTAIN HOME," FOR A TEN-POEM CONTEST AT KONRENJI

The loneliness
of life
      here in my lodging
I had expected;
but, ah,
       how I tire of hearing
the wind in the pines
          at my eaves!*

*sabishisa wa / omoishi mama no / yado nagara
nao kikiwaburu / noki no matsukaze*

---

*The word "pine" (J. *matsu*) is a homophone for the word "wait." The speaker thus complains that the sound of the wind in the pines makes him realize that he is really waiting for someone to visit.

"PINES AT A MOUNTAIN COTTAGE,"
WRITTEN AT THE HOME OF THE MIKOHIDARI
LAY-MONK MAJOR COUNSELOR [TAMESADA]

This hut of mine
is so far
            from the capital
that no one visits;
yet still
            the wind blows
                        in vain
through the pine trees
            at my eaves.*

*waga io wa / miyako o tōmi / hito mo kode
itazura ni fuku / noki no matsukaze*

---

*An allusive variation on *Man'yōshū* 51, by Shiki no Miko (written
after the capital had been transferred from Asuka Palace to Fujiwara
Palace): Winds of Asuka / that flutter the long sleeves / of the court
maidens / are so far from the capital / that they blow here in vain
(uneme no / sode fukikaesu / asukakaze / miyako o tōmi / itazura
ni fuku).

WRITTEN AT HIS NINNAJI COTTAGE

A sad thing it is
to hear it
            in company
with the world's woes—
a storm
            in the mountains
so near
            to the capital.*

yo no usa o / soete kiku koso / kanashikere
miyako ni chikaki / yama no arashi ni

---

*Probably a reference to battles fought around the capital in asso-
ciation with the rebellion of Emperor Go-Daigo or subsequent
friction between the Northern and Southern Courts.

"LAMENT," FROM POEMS WRITTEN FOR DHARMA EYE KEN'YO

Had there been
         no place
in the mountain shadows
for me to flee to—
what would there be
         to console me
amid the world
         and its woes?*

nogarekite / sumu yamakage no / nakariseba
nani o ukiyo no / nagusame ni sen

---

*An allusion to *Fūgashū* 609, by Senshi Naishinnō (written on a night when the moon was full): And were it not / for the bright autumn moon / shining in my heart, / what would there be to console me / amid the world and its woes? (kokoro sumu / aki no tsuki dani / nakariseba / nani o ukiyo no / nagusame ni semu).

80

In my mountain home
where alone
      I bear the pain
of loneliness—
the years go
      passing by,
and no one
      comes to visit.*

*sabishisa ni / taete sumu mi no / yamazato wa
toshi furu mama ni / tou hito mo nashi*

---

*An allusive variation on *Shin kokinshū* 627, by Saigyō (topic un-
known): Ah, such loneliness— / if there were only someone / to
bear it with me. / Side by side we'd put our huts / for winter in a
mountain village (sabishisa ni / taetaru hito no / mata mo are na /
iori narabemu / fuyu no yamazato).

"LAMENT," FROM A HUNDRED-POEM
SEQUENCE WRITTEN IN THE ŌCHŌ ERA
[1311]

To prattle on,
complaining
              about the woes
of one's situation—
that is to betray
                  the heart
that cast the world
                  aside.

to ni kaku ni / ukimi o nao no / nageku koso
suteshi ni tagau / kokoro narikere

"LAMENT, RELATED TO 'OLD TREE,'" WRITTEN WHEN PEOPLE WERE DRAWING FOR TOPICS*

What shall I do
for protection
                from the blows
of these harsh winds?
Now the old oaks
                in the groves
are completely dead and gone.†

araki kaze / fusegu tayori o / ikaga sen
oiki no hahaso / kuchihatenu ma ni

Dai o saguru, an informal competition in which poems were composed extemporaneously on topics chosen at random.

†The first two syllables of the word for "oaks," *hahaso,* are homophones with the word for "mother." An allusion to a Chinese poem: "The trees would be still, but the winds never stop; children would be nurtured, but their parents can't stay." Also probably an echo of a famous poem in *Genji monogatari* in which the mother of Kiritsubo expresses her worries for Genji, whom after his mother's death she compares to bush clover exposed to harsh winds (*Genji monogatari,* volume 12 of *Shin nihon koten bungaku zenshū* [Tokyo: Shoggakan, 1970], p. 110; Murasaki Shikibu, *The Tale of Genji,* trans. Edward Seidensticker [New York: Knopf, 1976], p. 11).

83

"LAMENT NEAR DAWN"

The awful sadness
of all
     that has happened to me
until this moment—
awake,
     as my night grows late,
that's when it comes to mind.

omoikoshi / mi no aramashi no / kanashisa mo
waga yo fukeyuku / nezame ni zo shiru

ON THE IDEA OF "TEARS OF GRIEF,"
WRITTEN AT KONRENJI

So old am I now
that I myself
             don't even know
all of the reasons
that the tears
             come falling down,
drenching
             the sleeves of my robe.

oinureba / nani yue otsuru / namida to mo
ware sae shirade / nururu sode kana

85

Ah, the past, we think—
but what
        we look back upon
was the same world
              of woe—
remembered fondly,
          perhaps,
because we hadn't yet
           grown old.

*mukashi tote / onaji ukiyo o / shinobu kana
toshi no oinu o / omoide ni shite*

86

"REMINISCING," FROM POEMS COMPOSED
WHEN SHŌJŌ CAME TO VISIT

Less substantial
than a dream
    were the months and years
that passed me by.
How is it that
    all together
they add up
    to make me old?

*yume yori mo / hakanaku sugishi / toshitsuki no
ikade ka oi no / kazu to naruran*

"REMINISCING"

If all that had passed
we could
            never remember—
what would help us,
                        then,
for even a moment
                        to forget
the troubles of old age?

koshikata o / omoiidezu wa / shibashi dani
nani ni ka oi no / uki o wasuremu

88

If one gave no thought
to the day
      one would return
to one's native home,
then there would be
        no reason
to make haste
     along the way.

furusato ni / kaerikon hi o / omowazu wa
tabiyuku michi o / isogazaramashi

89

ON "TRAVELER'S LAMENT," FROM A FIVE-
POEM SEQUENCE REQUESTED BY JAKU'E

So be it, then!
I will not bemoan
        the world's woes—
for as I push on
through fields,
      or mountains,
             everywhere
I find people
    just living.

yo no naka o / yoshi ya nagekaji / wakeyukeba
no ni mo yama ni mo / hito wa sumikeri

90

What can one say
about
      the lengthy partings
in this world of men?
The geese
        that left in the haze
at least now
          have come again.*

*hito no yo no / nagaki wakare o / ikaga sen
kasumite inishi / kari wa kinikeri*

---

*An allusive variation on *Kokinshū* 210, an anonymous poem: The
wild geese that left, / fading away into the haze / spreading in
springtime / now are calling out again / above the mists of autumn
(harugasumi / kasumite inishi / karigane wa / ima zo naku naru /
akigiri no ue ni). Wild geese fly back to the continent each spring,
after spending the winter in Japan.

WHEN HE VISITED HIS MOTHER'S GRAVE
ON A DAY OF FALLING SNOW

To think of her
down there,
              underneath the moss—
that was sad enough.
And now she is
              deeper still,
buried here
              beneath the snow.*

*omoiyaru / koke no shita dani / kanashiki ni
fukaku mo yuki no / nao uzumu kana*

---

*An echo of *Shin kokinshū* 796, by Fujiwara no Shunzei (written in the autumn, after Teika's mother had passed on and he went to visit her grave, staying that night in a nearby temple): I come so seldom, / and yet how sad in the night / sounds the wind in the pines. / And she, there beneath the moss— / does she too hear it, endlessly? (mare ni kuru / yowa mo kanashiki / matsukaze o / taezu ya koke no / shita ni kikuram).

WRITTEN AFTER THE PASSING OF
THE TOJI'IN POSTHUMOUS MINISTER OF
THE LEFT [TAKAUJI]

Just what can it be
that makes them cry
                    so loudly?
But, ah, of course:
cicadas would know
                    how empty
is this world
            of the cicada shell.*

*ne ni tatete / nageku wa nani zo / utsusemi no
munashiki yo to wa / shiranu mono ka wa*

---

*The shell shed by the cicada was a conventional symbol for
ephemerality.

93

Never
        did they know
they had left
            their tracks behind—
my friends, the plovers.*
In what bay,
            how far away
will they be
            living now?

*todomeoku / ato o mo shirade / tomochidori
ika naru kata no / ura ni sumuran*

Chidori, a small waterfowl associated with winter scenes whose call was often cast as a beckoning to companions. "Tracks" refers to writings.

"PRATYEKABUDDHA"*

Deep in the mountains,
I gaze up
        at the moon
shining in the clear—
leaves on the trees
           abandoned
to the enticing
        of the winds.

*okuyama ni / nagamuru tsuki wa / harenikeri
konoha o sasou / kaze ni makasete*

---

*J. engaku, a state of enlightenment arrived at independently of a master, symbolized in this poem by the moon shining clear after the speaker stops worrying about the leaves.

ON "SPRING RAIN," WRITTEN AT THE
HOUSE OF THE SHOGUN [YOSHIAKIRA]

A faint snowfall,
leaving nothing
              on the ground;
then from a clear sky
—barely "falling" at all—
the first rains
              of spring.

awayuki no / tsumorade hareshi / sora yori mo
furu to shi mo naki / haru no ame kana

ON "BLOSSOMS AT A BARRIER GATE,"
WRITTEN WHEN THE DANSHŌ PRINCE
VISITED SAIKE'EN, AT A TIME WHEN THE
BLOSSOMS WERE IN FULL BLOOM

At Meeting Hill,
the guards
        who bar the way
can relax a while—
their task of halting
             passersby
left
    to the cherry blossoms.*

*ausaka no / seki no sekimori / itoma are ya /
hito o todomuru / hana ni makasete*

---

*An allusive variation on *Shin kokinshū* 67, by Shōmyō (b. 1112)
(written on "Seedlings in the Rain," at the house of Lord
Kiyosuke): When the rain comes down, / the men working in the
fields / can relax a while— / their task of flooding seedling beds /
left to the sky above (ame fureba / oda no masurao / itoma are ya
/ nawashiromizu o / sora ni makasete).

"BLOSSOMS, IN SOLITUDE," FOR A HUNDRED-POEM SEQUENCE ON BLOSSOMS AT THE SEIKANJI

What a solace
from the loneliness
          of my home
are cherries in full bloom—
bringing those
          who never visit
calling at my door.

sabishisa o / nagusamu yado no / hana sakari
higoro oto senu / hito no touran

98

ON "BLOSSOM FRIENDS," WRITTEN WHEN
THE REIZEI CONSULTANT [TAMEHIDE]
WAS COMPOSING POEMS AT THE COTTAGE
OF REN'A

Friends I used to see
I shunned
        in taking up life
in my mountain home—
where the blossoms
            every spring
acquaint me again
        with men.*

*mukashi mishi / tomo o ba itou / yamazato mo
hana yue hito ni / naruru haru kana*

---

*People come to see the blossoms every spring.

ON "REMINISCENCE, RELATED TO
'BLOSSOMS,'" WRITTEN WHEN THE
REGENT [YOSHIMOTO] CAME TO VISIT

I cannot claim
that it does not
                    trouble my thoughts—
the sight
        of blossoms
that so increase
                one's longing
for things of long ago.*

*monoomoi / nashi to wa iwaji / hana mireba
itodo mukashi no / koishisa zo masu*

---

*An allusive variation on *Kokinshū* 52, by the Former Chancellor
[Fujiwara no Yoshifusa] (804–872) (on seeing an arrangement of
blossoms in a vase in the apartments of the Somedono Empress):
As the years go by / I just keep growing older— / that is true, and
yet / when I gaze upon blossoms / how untroubled are my
thoughts! (toshi fureba / yowai wa oinu / shika wa aredo / hana o
shi mireba / monoomoi mo nashi). Also probably an allusion to
Shin kokinshū 782, by Fujiwara no Saneyori: On seeing maiden-
flowers after the death of Lord Rengi's mother: My heart as I gaze
/ upon these maidenflowers / finds no solace— / so do they in-
crease one's longing / for autumns of long ago (ominaeshi / miru
ni kokoro wa / nagusamade / itodo mukashi no / aki zo koishiki).

ON "FALLING BLOSSOMS," FOR A THREE-
POEM SEQUENCE AT THE HOME OF THE
KAJII PRINCE OF THE SECOND RANK

Not satisfied
with enticements
   in the branches,
the storm winds
    blow on
over the grounds
    of a garden
strewn with fallen
     blossoms.*

*kozue yori / sasou ni akade / sakurabana
chirishiku niwa ni / arashi fuku nari*

*An allusion to *Shikashū* 142, by Minamoto no Sukemichi (d. 1060)
(written on "Fallen Leaves," for a poem contest at his house): Un-
satisfied / seeing them on the branches, / I gaze on the leaves /
strewn about the garden grounds— / not yet sweeping them away
(kozue nite / akazarishikaba / momijiba no / chirishiku niwa o /
harawade zo miru).

101

ON "BLOSSOMS AT AN INN," FROM AMONG
POEMS WRITTEN WHEN THE MIKOHIDARI
LAY-MONK MAJOR COUNSELOR [TAMESADA]
CAME TO VISIT

This spring,
        in moonlight
on a mountain path
           I rest
from my travels;
and there,
        in the waking world,
I see blossoms
        scattering.*

kono haru wa / tsuki ni yamaji no / tabine shite
utsutsu ni hana no / chiru o miru kana

---

*An echo of *Kokinshū* 117, by Ki no Tsurayuki (composed when he
was staying at a mountain temple): On a spring hillside / I took
lodging for the night; / and as I slept / the blossoms kept on fall-
ing— / even in the midst of my dreams (yadori shite / haru no
yamabe ni / netaru yo wa / yume no uchi ni mo / hana zo chiri-
keru).

ON "MOUNTAIN AZALEAS," COMPOSED
WHEN THE NIJŌ CONSULTANT [TAMETADA]
CAME TO VISIT

On Evergreen Hill
I come upon
            a color
not seen
            last autumn
here in the mountain groves—
red azaleas,
            between stones.*

*tokiwayama / aki wa mizarishi / kurenai no
iro ni idenuru / iwatsutsuji kana*

---

*An allusive variation on *Kokinshū* 362, an anonymous poem:
Though autumn comes, / there is no change in color / on Evergreen
Hill— / until leaves from elsewhere / are lent by the passing wind
(aki kuredo / iro mo kawaranu / tokiwayama / yoso no momiji o
/ kaze zo kashikeru).

103

"CUCKOO, LATE AT NIGHT," WRITTEN AT
THE HOME OF THE TOJI'IN POSTHUMOUS
MINISTER OF THE LEFT [TAKAUJI]

As if to declare,
"Only those
            who waited up
may hear my song!"
—the first call of the cuckoo*
comes
        just once,
                late in the night.

*shiite matsu / hito nomi kike to / hototogisu
fukete ya morasu / hatsune naru ran*

---

*The cuckoo, a harbinger of summer, was notoriously parsimoni-
ous with his calls.

"RICE SPROUTS," FROM A FIFTY-POEM SEQUENCE AT THE HOME OF THE LAY-MONK PRINCE OF THE SECOND RANK

Both far and near
along
      riverbank paddies,
the boats pull in—
taking on
      rice sprouts
           picked
by the villagers of Uji.

ochikochi no / kawazoioda ni / fune yosete
sanae toru nari / uji no satobito

"FIREFLIES"

As evening comes on,
they too
          begin their slow burn:
low down
          in the smoke
of mosquito smudges*—
fireflies
          darting about.

yūgure wa / onore mo moete / kayaribi no
keburi no shita ni / tobu hotaru kana

---

*Burned to ward off mosquitoes.

ON THE LINE "AUTUMN'S VOICE—CARRYING
A BURDEN OF RAIN,"* FROM A HUNDRED-
POEM SEQUENCE USING LINES FROM OLD
COLLECTIONS AS TOPICS

Wind passing over
lotus leaves
   out on a pond—
dewdrops cascading;
in autumn,
   the cooling sound
of rain coming down.

kaze wataru / ike no hasu no ha / tsuyu ochite
aki ni suzushiki / ame no oto kana

---

*A line from the Chinese poet Bo Juyi (722–846). See Inada
Toshinori, *Waka shitennō no Kenkyū* (Tokyo: Kasama Shoin, 1999),
p. 869.

ON "SUMMER COOL," FROM A THREE-POEM
SEQUENCE COMPOSED AT THE HOUSE OF
THE NAKAZONO LAY-MONK CHANCELLOR
[KINKATA]

More than anywhere
it is here
      that one feels the cool
of the passing winds—
where the sun cannot break through
beneath the trees
        in the garden.

izuku yori / suzushiki kaze no / kayouran
hikage wa moranu / niwa no kokage ni

108

FROM A FIFTY-POEM SEQUENCE AT THE
HOME OF THE LAY-MONK PRINCE OF THE
SECOND RANK

In my old home town,
no one comes
         to visit.
—the leaves
         on the reeds
left alone
         to make replies
to the tidings
         of the wind.*

*furusato wa / tou hito mo nashi / ogi no ha no
kaze ni kotauru / oto bakari shite*

---

*An allusive variation on *Kokinshū* 205, an anonymous poem: As
the crickets cry / in my mountain village / in the growing dusk, /
no one comes to visit— / except for the passing wind (higurashi
no / naku yamazato no / yūgure wa / kaze yori hoka ni / tou hito
mo nashi).

ON "BLOSSOMS ON GRASSES IN A
TRANQUIL GARDEN," WRITTEN WHEN
PEOPLE WERE COMPOSING POEMS AT THE
GRAVE OF THE POSTHUMOUS THIRD RANK
AT KYŌGOKU, ON THE FIRST ANNIVERSARY
OF HER DEATH

And if not
             for those
who come to visit
                 the grave
at her former home—
how overgrown, then,
                        would be
this clump
          of pampas fronds?*

*furusato ni / ato tou hito no / kayowazu wa /
hitomura susuki / nao ya shigeran*

---

*An allusive variation on *Kokinshū* 853, by Miharu Arisuke (after the death of Fujiwara no Toshimoto, no one was living in the chambers he had occupied as Middle Captain of the Right Guards; looking in on the place late at night on the way back from an event, he saw that the front garden was abandoned and overgrown and, thinking of the past when he had served there, he composed this): That clump of pampas / that you planted long ago / has spread to become / a field thick with cricket calls / and ever encroaching grasses (kimi ga ueshi / hitomura susuki / mushi no ne no / shigeki nobe to mo / narinikeru kana).

110

"HEARING A DEER BEFORE THE MOON,"
FROM A THREE-POEM SEQUENCE FOR THE
DANSHŌ PRINCE

Late into the night
I wait for one
            who doesn't come,
when in the moonlight
comes the sound
            of a deer calling—
also longing
            for his mate?

konu hito no / mataruru yowa no / tsukikage ni
sazo tsuma koi no / shika mo nakuran

"MOONLIGHT SHINING IN BLOSSOMS ON
THE GRASSES," FROM A THREE-POEM
SEQUENCE AT THE HOME OF THE SHOGUN
[YOSHIAKIRA]

The failing red hue
of dewdrops
            on bush clover
fades further into white—
jewels
        buffed to a high sheen
by the light of the moon.

murasaki ni / utsurou hagi no / tsuyu no iro o
mata shiratama to / migaku tsuki kana

"MIST ABOVE A RIVER," FROM A FIFTEEN-POEM SEQUENCE OF THE FORMER REGENT

Winds out on the river
cast over
    the cresting waves
a sheet of morning mist—
and floating above,
    down river
comes a firewood barge
    from Uji.*

*kawakaze no / nami ni fukishiku / asagiri ni
ukite zo kudaru / uji no shibafune*

---

*An allusive variation on *Shin kokinshū* 169, by Jakuren (presented as part of a fifty-poem sequence): Toward what harbor / spring goes when it fades away / one cannot know— / a barge of firewood falling / into River Uji's haze (kurete yuku / haru no minato wa / shiranedomo / kasumi ni otsuru / uji no shibabune).

"THE BEGINNING OF WINTER"

Mountains
          all around
are as they were
                yesterday,
in autumn colors;
then, as if to say,
                "Stay no more!"
come the withering
                winds.

yama wa mina / kinō no mama no / aki no iro o
nokosaji to fuku / kogarashi no kaze

ON "COLD GRASSES," FROM A THREE-POEM
VOTIVE SEQUENCE OFFERED TO KITANO
SHRINE BY THE FORMER REGENT

In the frost-withered
pampas grass
      of Mano Moor
the wind turns
      chill—
leaving only
      the memory
of autumn
      in my mind.*

*shimogare no / mano no kayahara / kaze saete
omokage ni nomi / nokoru aki kana*

---

*An allusive variation on *Gosenshū* 132, by Ōshikōchi no Mitsune
(on seeing cherry blossoms scattering): The time went by / and
suddenly the blossoms / had scattered and gone— / leaving only
the memory / of their colors in my mind (itsu no ma ni / chiri-
hatenuran / sakurabana / omokage ni nomi / iro o misetsutsu).

**"FROST ON A BRIDGE," WRITTEN WHEN
PEOPLE WERE CHOOSING TOPICS AT THE
HOME OF THE REGENT [YOSHIMOTO]**

This morning
           still
there are no footprints
               from people
coming and going;
as frosted now
           as in the night
are the planks of Just-So Bridge.

*kesa wa mada / hito no yukiki no / ato mo nashi
yo no ma no shimo no / mama no tsugibashi*

"FROZEN INLET"

Only
　　　from far back
comes the sound
　　　　　　　of rowing;
into the ice-bound
inlets
　　　around Mano Bay
not a boat
　　　　approaches.

oku ni kogu / oto bakari shite / mano no ura no
kōru irie wa / yoru fune mo nashi

117

"COAL FIRE AT DAWN," WRITTEN WHEN PEOPLE WERE COMPOSING VOTIVE POEMS FOR KITANO SHRINE

Had I not heard
the tolling
           of the dawn bell*
I would not
            have known
how cold
        was the frosty night
away from
          my coal fire.

akatsuki no / kane o kikazu wa / shimo sayuru
yowa to mo shiraji / uzumibi no moto

---

*The first bell of the day at Buddhist temples, calling monks to prayer.

ON "SNOW," COMPOSED FOR A SINGLE-DAY
THOUSAND-VERSE SEQUENCE AT THE
HOUSE OF THE MINISTER OF POPULAR
AFFAIRS [TAMEFUJI]

In my mountain home—
a snowfall
        one wants to save
from trails of footprints.
How could one claim
        to welcome
a visitor who comes today?*

yamazato wa / atozukegataku / furu yuki ni
kyō komu hito to / matare yawa suru

---

*An allusive variation on *Shūishū* 251, by Taira no Kanemori (topic
unknown): In my mountain home, / snow has fallen over all— /
including my path. / One can only pity the plight / of a visitor
who comes today (yamazato wa / yuki furitsumite / michi mo nashi
/ kyō komu hito o / aware to wa mimu).

"SNOW AT SHORESIDE"

On Tago Bay
the high peak
             of Mount Fuji
appears
          in shadow form:
waves and all
               becoming one
with the white
             of falling snow.*

*tago no ura ya / fuji no takane no / kage miete
nami mo hitotsu ni / fureru shirayuki*

---

*An echo of *Man'yōshū* 318, by Yamabe no Akahito: At Tago Bay
/ I came out, and looked afar— / to see the pure white / of Mount
Fuji's lofty peak, / amid a flurry of snow (tago no ura yu / uchiidete
mireba / mashiro ni zo / fuji no takane ni / yuki wa furikeru).

"SNOW AT SHORESIDE"

A winter so cold
that the snow is
                    piling up
at harborside—
where
        left by the bank to rot
is a cast-off
            fishing boat.

*fuyu samumi / yuki zo furitsumu / minatoe ni
kuchite nokoreru / ama no sutebune*

FROM A FIFTY-POEM SEQUENCE FOR THE
LAY-MONK PRINCE OF THE SECOND RANK

"When the snow falls
in the garden,"
                    he said to me—
but he doesn't come;
so busy a time
                    it is
at the end
        of the year.*

*niwa no yuki ni / furaba to iishi / hito wa kode
isogu mo shiruki / toshi no kure kana*

---

*An allusive variation on a poem by Jien from the *Kenpō yonen
hyakushu* (also *Shin shūishū* 654): "When first snow falls / in the
garden," he said to me— / but he doesn't come; / to no purpose,
then, the clouds clear / from the evening sky (hatsuyuki no / furaba
to iishi / hito wa kode / munashiku haruru / yūgure no sora).

"YEAR'S END," WRITTEN AT THE HOUSE
OF UNKEN

No surprise will I feel—
but think of him
                as some old man
I don't even know.
Even if the year
                does end
for the face
                in the mirror.*

*odorokade / shiranu okina ni / nashihaten
kagami no kage wa / toshi kurenu to mo*

---

*An allusive variation on *Shūishū* 565, an anonymous *sedōka:* There in the mirror / I come face to face with someone / who stares back at me, / feeling as if / I am meeting an old man / that I do not even know (masukagami / soko naru kage ni / mukaiite miru / toki ni koso / shiranu okina ni / au kokochi sure).

"SECRET LOVE"

And if she should ask,
"Look how drenched through
                        they are—
the sleeves of your robe!
What is it
            that has made them so?"
how am I to reply?

kaku bakari / nani yue nururu / tamoto zo to
kimi shi mo towaba / ikaga kotaen

ON "LOVE, RELATED TO 'CLOUD,'"
COMPOSED WHEN FUJIWARA MOTOYO CAME
TO COMPOSE POEMS

In a mountain's shade,
below
      winds
           that dissipate
a storm's white clouds—
what has not yet
            cleared away
is the darkness
        of my thoughts.

*yamakage ni / kaze no fukishiku / shirakumo no
shita ni harenu wa / omoi narikeri*

"ONE-SIDED LOVE," COMPOSED AT THE
HOUSE OF THE SHOGUN [YOSHIAKIRA]

I will not
            call it
merely his cruelty—
but just regard it
as the sad plight
                    of one
with no pledge
                from a former life.*

tsurashi to mo / hito o ba iwade / saki no yo ni
chigiri naki mi no / uki ni nasu kana

---

*An allusive variation on *Kin'yōshū* 438, by Saki no Chūgu no
Kazusa: Not realizing / that it must be a bond carried / from a
former life, / how quickly I dismissed it / as the cruelty of his heart
(saki no yo no / chigiri o shirade / hakanaku mo / hito o tsurashi
to / omoikeru kana).

126

"CLOSE LOVE," COMPOSED WHEN THE
REIZEI CONSULTANT [TAMEHIDE] WAS
COMPOSING POEMS AT SAIKE'EN

A couple in turmoil
is an image
       reflected
back from a mirror:
there you appear
       face to face
but nothing passes
       between.

uki naka wa / kagami ni utsuru / kage nare ya
miyu to wa suredo / koto mo kayowazu

"WAITING FOR LOVE"

Ah, the futility
of putting trust
in pledges
that turn out to be lies!
And less reason
is there to wait
on an evening
never promised.

itsuwari o / tanomu dani koso / hakanaki ni
chigiranu kure no / nani mataruran

"LOVE, NO MORE SECRET"

"Never let it out!"
was his vow to me
                    back then,
but what will happen now?
For with all that
                    in his heart
still his feelings
                    have changed.

morasu na to / chigirishi sue mo / ika naran
sanagara kawaru / hito no kokoro ni

129

"MEETING AGAIN AFTER SEPARATING"

A bridge
      of wood planks
that in the past
         had collapsed
may lead to
       danger
for those who try to
          go on
and cross over it
      again.

todae seshi / maki no tsugibashi / tsugite nao
watasu ni tsukete / sue zo ayauki

"MOUNTAIN HOME"

Once, I was sure
that I would find
                    the loneliness
more than I could bear.
Until,
        by getting used to it,
I got used to
              the mountain depths.*

*taete yo mo / araji to omoishi / sabishisa mo
narureba naruru / yama no oku kana*

---

*An echo of *Sankashū* 937, a famous poem by Saigyō (topic un-
known): I have given up / all hope of having visitors / in my
mountain home. / If not for solitude, / how dismal my life would
be! (*tou hito mo / omoitaetaru / yamazato no / sabishisa naku wa
/ sumiukaramashi*).

ON "MOUNTAIN HOME," COMPOSED WHEN
THE OGURA CONSULTANT-MIDDLE CAPTAIN
[SANENA] CAME TO VISIT

When guests from Miyako
take their leave,
                then even more
than before
            they came
will my home in the mountains
be a place
            of loneliness.

miyakobito / kaeraba nao ya / yamazato wa
towarenu yori mo / sabishikaramashi

132

"LIVING IN TRANQUILITY," COMPOSED
WHEN THE REIZEI CONSULTANT [TAMEHIDE]
CAME TO VISIT

I need
  seek out
no house
   of retirement.
Wherever one lives
in the days
   of one's old age
will be a place
    of solitude.

kakurega mo / ima wa tazuneji / izuku ni mo
oite sumu koso / shizuka narikere

133

ON "DAY'S END ON THE WATER"

Daylight is fading—
let's find mooring
              for our boat!
Off there
        where the light
of fishing fires is glowing
must be the homes
              of fishermen.

kurenikeri / fune ya tomemashi / isaribi no
kage miru kata wa / ama zo sumuran

"REMINISCING AT DAWN," COMPOSED AT THE HOME OF THE FORMER REGENT

With never a thought
for how close I am
                    to the end,
why is it
        that the past
is all
    I can think about—
an old man,
            awake in the night?

yukusue no / chikaki o shirade / mukashi nomi
nado shinobaruru / oi no nezame wa

LINKED VERSE COUPLETS

135

Yesterday, and then today
　the snow just keeps on falling.

In pools, in rapids,
the waters have frozen over—
making not a sound.

kinō mo kyō mo / yuki zo nao furu;
fuchi mo se mo / kōreba mizu no / oto taete

Thinking to read letters,
I end up sleepless, all night.

Not in a dream,
I find myself meeting again
    those of long ago.

fumi o yomu tote / yoru mo nerarezu;
yume narade / mukashi no hito ni / ainikeri

137

High up, there in mid-sky—
the moon on an autumn night.

Nobody visits
  and I go to see no one—
night growing long.

nakazora ni naru / aki no yo no tsuki;
hito mo kozu / waga mi mo towade / fukenikeri

Not two, not three—but one
  alone is the Buddha's Law.

On shore we wait
  for the boat to row back
    and take us across.*

futatsu mo mitsu mo / naki minori kana;
kogikaeru / hodo o ya matamu / watashibune

---

*"Rowing to the far shore" was a common metaphor for achieving enlightenment or rebirth in the Pure Land.

How long shall we gaze upon
   the blossoms and the moon?

Morning glories abloom
   on a wattled fence, dew laden
     in the light of dawn.*

hana to tsuki to mo / itsu made ka mimu;
asagao no / kakiho no tsuyu no / akebono ni

---

*The second verse answers the question of the first in two ways:
first, by providing a concrete setting for the scene—dew on flowers,
sparkling in the moonlight at dawn—and, second, by suggesting
that such beauties do not last long.

Completely frozen over
    and yet—still the waves rise.

Moonlight resting
    on the tips of pampas plumes
        heavy with fall dew.*

kōredomo nao / nami wa tachikeri;
tsuki yadoru / obana ga sue no / aki no tsuyu

---

*In the link, the "waves" become the pampas fronds, swaying under a burden of moonlit dew.

Even those beyond feeling
   are not without friends.

In mountain streams
   water flows over the shadows
     of rocks and trees.*

kokoro naki ni mo / tomo wa arikeri;
yamamizu ya / iwaki no kage o / nagaruran

---

*The friends "beyond feeling"—in other words, not human—are
the rocks and trees, whose shadows act as companions, side by side.

It passes over the mountains—
then the wind is heard no more.

When the waterfall
  in the end becomes a pond—
there is no more sound.*

yama suginureba / kaze mo kikoezu;
takikawa mo / ike ni narite wa / oto mo nashi

---

*A Buddhist allegory, suggesting the transmutability of all things.
Just as the wind fades off into empty sky, so does the spray of a
waterfall become the standing water of a pond.

In the south and in the north,
the snow has kept on falling.

So cold the sound
—in the morning, in the evening—
of the valley wind.*

*minami mo kita mo / yuki wa furikeri;
oto samuki / ashita yūbe no / tanikaze ni*

---

*Here the "opposites" of morning and evening complement the south and the north, with the valley wind serving as the transporting agent of the snow.

144

In the night, the snow itself
  provides us with our light.

'Til break of day
  the moon still remains—
but casting no rays.*

yuki koso yoru no / hikari narikere;
akuru made / tsuki wa nokoredo / kage mo nashi

---

*Here it is the faint dawn moonlight on the snow that creates light
in the darkness.

Still in the fickle world,
I find myself lingering on.

Every single morning
   blooms appear on morning glories,
day adding to day.*

ada naru yo ni mo / nagaraenikeri;
asagoto ni / saku asagao no / hi kazuete

---

*The morning glory is a conventional symbol for ephemerality,
suggesting that even those who "linger on" will not do so for long.

One leaves, and then the mountains
of Miyako remain no more.

Out on the boatway
it is from the sea that the moon
rises into sight.*

yukeba miyako no / yama mo nokorazu;
funaji ni wa / umi yori izuru / tsuki o mite

---

*Here the link takes the first verse as a riddle: How is it that the mountains of the capital disappear, when all roads out of the city lead through the mountains? The answer is that the mountains disappear into the night, especially so when one leaves not by land but by sea.

Withered by frost,
a little skiff parts the reeds,
rowing away.

Between waves, the new day breaks
   on the snow of distant hills.

shimogare no / ashiwakeobune / kogiidete;
namima ni akuru / yuki no tōyama

If only for a moment, where
  can I hide myself away?

When the cherries bloom,
there is no mountain recess
  without its visitors.*

shibashi izuku ni / mi o kakusamashi;
hanazakari / towarenu yama no / oku mo nashi

---

*Here the link provides a speaker for the first verse—a mountain recluse who cannot escape company while the cherry trees are in bloom.

In unison with the flute—
the plucking of *koto* strings.

Grass cutters return
  from work in the evening
    with the pining wind.*

fue ni awasete / koto ya hikuran;
kusakari no / kaeru yūbe no / matsu no kaze

---

*In the link, the flute is played by one of the grass cutters on his
way home, with the sound of the zither coming on the wind in
the pines.

In far-off mountains,
from a peak a bell rings—
ever so faintly.

In haze, a new day breaks
over a cedar grove.*

yama tōki / onoe no kane wa / kasuka nite;
kasumite akuru / sugi no muradachi

---

*The link here provides a concrete setting for the images of the
first verse—the temple located now in a cedar grow, the bell an-
nouncing dawn ringing faintly through spring haze.

FROM A FROG AT THE BOTTOM OF A WELL

SELECTIONS

The late master Tameyo said: "Shunzei's style is that of mystery and depth,[1] which is most difficult to achieve; Teika's style is that of profound meaning,[2] which is difficult to master. Hence it is the style of Lay-Monk Minister of Popular Affairs [Tameie] that you should learn." This is a profound insight.

According to the late master Tameyo, Tameie said this: "My late father's poems were superb, of course, but if descendants who know nothing about poetry put them into anthologies indiscriminately, there are many bad poems among them. My own poems are stupid by comparison, but even if descendants who know nothing about poetry should put them in anthologies, I have taken care not to leave behind any poems that are all that bad."

The late master Tameyo said: "Nijō Norisada, Commander of the Left Guards, was a disciple of the Way who, on top of that, married into the family—as father-in-law to Tameuji—and became an intimate. Once during the chatting after a banquet, he declared how moved he was by poem by Teika, and how much it had impressed him:

> In the moonlight
>   of the dawn moon of the Long Month,
> rain showers come down—
> a bitter prospect for the leaves
>   whose hues will change tomorrow.[3]

*nagatsuki no / tsuki no ariake no / shigure yue
asu no momiji no / iro mo urameshi*

At this Tameie put down the saké cup he had been holding, anger showing in his face. "What could possibly be of interest in such a poem?" he said.

"I didn't mean to go that far," Norisada said. "I was just saying what I felt."

"You shouldn't be so quick to say something so offensive. True, Teika did put the poem in his *Hundred-Poem Contest*,[4] but the style of the thing is simply inappropriate.[5] Certainly it is not a poem that would be included in an imperial anthology," Tameie responded, most sternly. "I simply can't comprehend why you would praise such a poem," he is reported to have said.[6]

"It's inconceivable to me how the poem got put into *Gyokuyōshū*,"[7] the late master said. (A personal note: This poem is not in *Gyokuyōshū*.)[8]

Minister of Popular Affairs [Tamefuji] said: "You should get comments on your poems, as a way to avoid public embarrassment." On the topic "Willows Along the Road," Teika composed this poem for a poetry gathering at the imperial palace:

> Along the pathway,
> the willow trees in the fields

> are ablaze in green—
> in sympathy with a heart
> smoldering in envy?

michinobe no / nohara no yanagi / moesomete /
aware omoi no / keburikurabe ya

After Retired Emperor Go-Toba had looked over the poems from the event, he gave an order to the imperial palace prohibiting Teika from attendance at court. After some days, when he was allowed back into service, Teika made a special visit to Courtiers Hall and said, "For the benefit of the Way, one must feel that a command of this sort is most welcome." The masters of the past thought likewise—a lesson that we in later ages should learn well.[9]

Tamefuji said: "Retired Emperor Go-Toba once tossed one of the Teika's poems aside because he didn't understand it, yet later looked at it again and was very impressed, declaring it a work of deep meaning."[10] We should keep this in mind, and when looking at the poems of the masters of the past do so with special care.

Tamefuji said: "In a letter written to Reverend Jichin, Teika said, 'Saigyō hails me as Japan's number-one poet, but compared with my late father I'm not even a tenth as good.'"

Tamefuji said: "Ietaka was the son-in-law of Jakuren, along with whom he became a poetic disciple of Shunzei. According to Tameie, Shunzei noted of Ietaka, 'This young man is sure to become a sage in the future. When he comes to see me, he never asks about obscurities but always about the proper feeling one should have in composing poems,' and was very much impressed."

According to Saitō Mototo, Tsuchimikado'in Kosaishō said: "Among the poems of Ietaka there is none that is hard to understand. The poem

> Up on the slopes
>   at Takasago, the days
> when no stag calls out
>   have accumulated now—
> with white snow on the pines.[11]

> *takasago no / onoe no shika no / nakanu hi mo*
> *tsumorihatenuru / matsu no shirayuki*

for instance, is thought by some people to be difficult to understand. But it is only difficult if you think too much about it; the sense of the poem is easily comprehended if you just take it straightforwardly."

Someone said: "When poems for the *Shin chokusenshū*[12] were being selected, the compiler was in a quandary because there were no bright and lively[13] poems about plum blossoms. 'Surely there must be one among the poems of Ietaka,' he thought, and took a look. He found this poem and put it in:

> For how many leagues
>   do rays of light from the moon
> also bear the scent
>   of mountains of plum blossoms
> peaked with the breezes of spring?[14]

> *iku sato ka / tsuki no hikari mo / niouramu*
> *mume saku yama no / mine no harukaze*

The late master Tameyo told me this: "My late father's poem

> If anyone asks,
> I shall say I haven't seen it—

Tamatsu Isle,
where haze spreads over the inlet
in the dim light of spring dawn.[15]

hito towaba / mizu to ya iwan / tamatsushima
kasumu irie no / haru no akebono

was written for the *Poem Contest of the Kenchō Era.*[16] He
wrote it on the back of a sheet of recycled paper,[17] and then
showed it to my grandfather, Tameie. Next to where my fa-
ther had originally written, 'I shall say I *have seen it*—'
Tameie wrote, 'I shall say I *haven't seen it*—.' Though he
didn't understand exactly why, the author handed the poem
in as 'haven't seen.' "[18]

At the time of *The Shirakawa-dono Seven Hundred Poem Se-
quence,* the poem strip[19] of Shinkan was blown into the
stream by the wind on his way to the palace, so he presented
it on a towel, in a very unsightly state. One should be pre-
pared for such things.

Hafuribe Yukiuji said: "When I was a young man I met
Hafuribe Tadanari (a *Shin chokusenshū* author).[20] Because I
was consulting books[21] as I composed my poems, he told me,
'Look to the blue clouds when composing poems.[22] If you
rely too much on old poems now, you will never become a
fine poet.' "

The late master Tameyo said: "Tameie thought of Lord
Nobuzane as a poet without peer. At the time he was com-
piling *Shoku gosenshū,*[23] he wanted to put one of Nobuzane's
poems as the very first in the collection, so he wrote him a
message asking him to present ten poems on 'The Beginning
of Spring.' Nobuzane asked, 'What might the purpose of this
request be?' and didn't present any poems—a marvelous
show of humility.

"Once Nobuzane composed a set of one hundred po-
ems, which he asked Tameie to mark.[24] Among these was,

'in valley after valley / around Mount Hatsuse . . .' which he sent back with the comment 'Just like a mountain monk' written next to it. The evening of that same day, Nobuzane came calling at Chū'in.[25] Tameie received him, and said, 'Just what was the purpose of your visit?'

"'I have come because I was intrigued by your comment that my poem, "in valley after valley / around Mount Hatsuse," was just like a mountain monk,' was the reply."

What an elegant display of connoisseurship!

Lord Nobuzane had three daughters. They were all fine poets. Sōhekimon'in Shōshō was particularly outstanding. In his old age, Teika was moved so deeply by her poem

> There in his own voice
>   is the suffering that comes
>   when lovers must part—
> yet he doesn't seem to know,
> that rooster calling out.[26]

> *ono ga ne ni / tsuraki wakare no / ari to dani*
> *omoi mo shirade / tori ya nakuramu*

that he wrote her out a copy of *Kokinshū*[27] and sent it to her, with a postface inscribed, "To Shōshō, Sage Mother of the Nation, a true Adept of the Way. Copied out without concern for the failing powers of these old eyes."

Shōshō no Naishi was the one who died first, leaving the other two behind. Sōhekimon'in Shōshō took the tonsure in old age and lived at the old site of Hosshōji. The daughter of Taira no Chikakiyo came up from the East Country and, because Sōhekimon'in Shōshō was so famous, decided to go and see her at her dwelling at Hosshōji. Shōshō allowed her into the chapel and spoke to her through the sliding door.

"For you to come to my dwelling here in the deep grasses shows determination and admirable dedication to the

Way, and I would like to let you see my old countenance; but I fear I am not up to comparison with my poem 'There is in your own voice / something that makes me feel inadequate . . .' so I will demur," the old woman said. How gentle and refined a response! The daughter of Chikakiyo sent gifts from the hinterlands all the time and communicated by letter.

Ben no Naishi became a nun in old age and went into seclusion at a place called Augi, north of Sakamoto.[28] Retired Emperor Kameyama heard she was there and sent her topics for a Tanabata Meeting[29] by messenger. On the topic "Tanabata Robes," she wrote this:

> Autumn has come,
>   yet so narrow are my sleeves
>   laden with dew
>   that I have nothing I can lend
>   to the Tanabata Maiden.[30]

> *aki kite mo / tsuyu oku sode no / sebakereba*
> *tanabatazume ni / nani o kasamashi*

"How perfect," he thought, very moved, and corresponded with her frequently thereafter. An old man—a monk called Kōsen—who lived in Augi told this story.

The late master Tameyo said: "Back in the days when Tameie was a captain in the Gate Guards, a Bishop something-or-other was always coming to him with questions about poetry. After hearing that in poetry 'One should put truth above all else, and be sure that you adhere to logic,' he came some days later and said, 'I have written a poem according to your instructions the other day. I wonder if I've got it right.'

> The peak of Fuji
>   appears to be everywhere

the exact same shape—
whether from that side over there
or from this side over here.

fuji no yama / onaji sugata no / miyuru kana
anataomote mo / konataomote mo

'This isn't what should result from putting logic above all else,' Tameie said and broke out laughing."

The late master Tameyo said: "When I went to Tameie in order to receive the teachings on *Kokinshū*,[31] I brought Jō'i along with me, since I was used to using a monk as a scribe. 'I'm afraid something has come up, today,' Tameie said, and asked me to come again on a later date. Then privately he asked, 'Why did you bring someone with you?' Consequently, I came on a later day by myself and received the teachings."

The late master Tameyo said: "According to Tameie, 'You should compose poems like building a bridge, adjusting here and there so that it tilts neither left nor right.[32] You shouldn't just compose any way you like.' He also said, 'You should compose in the way you put up a tower. You don't put up a tower from the top down. In the same way that you build on top of a foundation, you should begin with the bottom half.'"

Lady Imadegawa'in Konoe no Tsubone said: "When the late Major Counselor [Korehira] had his children write poems, Lord Koreyori, Kakudō Shōnin, and Bishop Jitsu'i each composed many poems when still young. When I was in my ninth year, I was trying to compose on the topic, 'Ice on the Pond.' I noticed that my brothers were all writing about thin ice, and thinking that it would be boring to do the same thing, I wrote about 'thick ice, by the pondside.' Korehira liked this very much and said, 'This poem on thick ice is better than all the others; surely you will become a fine poet.' I have lived to greet five imperial anthologies, beginning with *Shoku kokinshū*,[33] and had many poems included in them[34]— indicating the foresight of my father's words."

She also composed Chinese poems, some of which were included in *Kensakushū*.[35] She kept Buddhist vows and was a Zen nun her entire life, never marrying. I have heard that she had read the *Lotus Sutra*[36] ten thousand times. She did not serve conspicuously at court. At the time of *Shoku kokinshū* she wore a sweet-flag ensemble[37] in the Fifth Month. She went to Imadegawa-In when the latter was empress; it was there she got the name Gon-dainagon and left without even getting out of the carriage.[38] Truly, "thick ice along the pondshore" was an outstanding line. She wrote beautiful and unusual things in every poem.

Tamefuji said: "Teika always used to say, 'When composing *uta,* you should be as if you were Major Counselor Kanemune, sitting in the Guards' Chamber[39] in formal robes, as if undertaking official business. Don't compose in the attitude of Sukemasa of the Third Rank, in informal hunting attire, as if about to go out hawking.' Tameie also used to say to everyone, 'This is what my late father said.' "[40]

Tamefuji said: "At the time of the *Shin chokusenshū,* hopefuls would present their poems, but seldom did they meet Teika's liking. 'Maybe it would be better if they sent me their cast-offs,' he declared.' "

Tamefuji said: "When Tameie was young, he was not proficient in the Way. Even though as the heir of his father and grandfather he had connections in the world, he made no progress. Having determined to abandon the lay world, he went to Hie Shrine to bid his leave. Around that same time, he visited Reverend Jichin to tell him of his intentions and say farewell.

"'How old are you?' the Reverend asked him.

"'Twenty-five,' Tameie replied.

"Then Jichin said, 'You are not yet at the age when things have become clear. You should put your decision off, and make it only after really accumulating experience in practice.'

"Following this advice, Tameie gave up his plan to leave the world and composed a thousand poems in five days. After finishing, he showed them to his father, who looked at the ten poems on 'The Beginning of Spring' and said, 'Well, if you can produce poems on "The Beginning of Spring" as good as these, then things look good.' After looking at all the poems, he told him to show them to Ietaka. In time, Tameie became Master of the Way and further improved on the heritage of his fathers—all thanks to Reverend Jichin."

In the Tokudaiji[41] there is a room called the Poetry Room.[42] It is in the western corner of the *shinden*.[43] This is where the Go-Tokudaiji Minister of the Left Sanesada met Saigyō.

The Ichijō Dharma Sign [Jō'i] said: "At the time *of The Six-Hundred Round Poem Contest of the Captain of the Left*,[44] members of the teams of the left and the right would go daily to make judgments, with each side writing its judgments down. Some days, there were those who didn't come, but Jakuren and Kenshō came every day, always arguing. Kenshō was a monk and wielded a *vajra* thunderbolt; Jakuren fought like a cobra lance.[45] It was the women of the palace who gave them these names."

Rokujō Arifusa said: "At the time of Retired Emperor Go-Toba, there were Persimmon and Chestnut factions.[46] The Persimmon faction favored ordinary poems, which were called 'poems of heart,' while the Chestnut faction favored madcap poems, called 'poems without heart.'[47] In the Persimmon group were the Go-Kyōgoku Lord, Reverend Jichin, and others who were among the finest poets of that time. In the Chestnut group were Lord Mitsuchika, Lord Muneyuki, Dharma Eye Taikaku, and so on. At the Poetry Offices in Minase, the Chestnut Chambers were on the other side of the courtyard. In the courtyard was a large pine tree. One delightful day when the wind was blowing, Revered Jichin wrote this poem and sent it to the poets of the 'no heart' faction:

> Those who have a heart
>   and those without any heart—
> is there between them
>   a difference in what they hear
>   from the wind in the garden pine?[48]

> *kokoro aru to / kokoro naki to ga / naka ni mata*
> *ika ni kike to ya / niwa no matsukaze*

"Lord Muneyuki wrote this in reply:

> Your lordship declares
>   that we haven't any heart—
> but one needs only ears
>   to listen to the wind blowing
>   in the pine by the eaves.[49]

> *kokoro nashi to / hito wa notamaedo / mimi shi areba*
> *kikisaburau zo / noki no matsukaze*

"'Rather witty, that "one needs only ears,"' the Retired Emperor declared, and had a good laugh. The Elder of the Minase Shrine (Shiichi Shōnin) told this story, which he said came from Minase of the Third Rank. The pine by the eaves of the Poetry Bureau was deeply favored by the Retired Emperor. Much later, he sent this poem, which he commanded to be tacked to the tree:

In days long ago,
there were blossoms that longed
    for their master.
But, alas, not this pine tree—
which gives no one a thought.[50]

inishie wa / hana zo aruji o / shitaikeru
matsu wa hito o mo / omowazarikeri

"After this poem was composed, the pine soon withered and died, so the story goes."

Tamefuji said: "Among Lord Ietaka's poems for the *Poetry Contest on a Distant Isle*[51] was this one:

Will I see this again?
Or will I not see it again?
White jewels of dew
    decorating the blossoms
        of bush clover in autumn.[52]

mata ya min / mata ya mizaran / shiratsuyu no
tama okishikeru / akihagi no hana

"Tameie said of this poem, 'Perhaps not inferior to Shunzei's

Will I see this again?
A hunt for cherry blossoms
    on Katano Moor—
petals of snow scattering
    in the first light of dawn.[53]

mata ya mimu / katano no mino no / sakuragari
hana no yuki chiru / haru no akebono

"'—although one might say that "Will I see this again?" makes "Or will I not see it again?" somewhat superfluous.'"

Tamefuji said: "When his father, Hidemune, died at the time of *Shin kokinshū*,[54] a poem on the topic 'Reminiscing, with Wind as an Image,' by Hidetō[55] was included. His older brother Hideyasu was envious, saying, 'If it meant gaining an honor such as that, I wouldn't begrudge having my head lopped off.'"

Tamefuji said: "Lord Tomoie was not as talented as his father, Akiie. Although he was rather untried in the Way, Teika took special interest in him. As he had not even received the teachings of his own house from his father, Teika taught him this and that and then praised him in one poem contest after another, saying that he was one of great ability. He was also favored with a number of poems in *Shin chokusenshū*.[56] Until well into his old age, Tomoie remained a disciple of our house, but after Teika's death his heart turned against us, and among the poems of his contribution to *The Hundred-Poem Sequences of the Hōji Era*[57] he wrote many not in keeping with the style of the house. Truly an ingrate."[58]

The Akai Prince said this: "The poem on 'The Moon Deep in the Mountains' by Tomoie,

> In the depths of night,
> I muse on about the past
>   of Mount Takano—
> the light of dawn still far away
>   here in the clear light of the moon.[59]

*mukashi omou / takano no yama no / fukaki yo ni
akatsuki tōku / sumeru tsukikage*

"impressed the Emperor Juntoku very much, who pronounced that he must give Tomoie something as a reward.

Since there was nothing else suitable about at the moment, he gave him ten tablets of fine paper. After receiving them, Tomoie hurried off to Sumiyoshi Shrine and presented the paper there as an offering to be used for prayer strips.[60] Everyone was very moved, so the story goes."

The late master Tameyo said: "Tameie said, 'When I am going to someone's house for a poetry gathering, I prepare one or two linked verse *hokku*,[61] on the usual *fushimono*—person, tree, boat, and so on.[62] Sometimes at the end of a gathering, suddenly someone says, "Let's do some linked verse," and you don't want to keep people waiting while you are coming up with a first verse.'"

The late master Tameyo said: "Once Tameie was going from Saga to his Reizei house, with Tamenori riding on the back of his carriage. Tamenori was criticizing the linked verse of his older brother, Tameuji. Tameie didn't say anything in reply, until he happened to see a dung wagon on the road and composed this verse:

> A skinny old ox
>   harnessed to a wagon
>   all heavy with dung.[63]

> *yaseushi ni / koeguruma o zo / kaketekeru*

"Tamenori squirmed around, but couldn't come up with a link. When they were about to get down at Reizei, Tameie said. 'You couldn't handle it, could you? Had it been your elder brother, he would have been able to come up with something.'"

Retired Emperor Go-Saga held a linked verse gathering at the Yoshida springs. Shōshō no Naishi was summoned and attended the emperor inside the blinds. Tameie, serving as messenger[64] for the lady, was under the eaves outside the blinds. Distracted by the sound of the waterfall in his ears, he couldn't hear well, and so couldn't get very interested in the *renga*. Lesser Captain Tamenori got some shrubbery from the mountain and put it under the waterfall so that you couldn't hear the water any more. Thereafter, everyone got into the *renga*, it is written in Ben no Naishi's journal.[65]

The Taira Middle Counselor, Lord Koresuke said: "Lord Enkō'in said, 'I have looked into all the various Ways,[66] and each is worthwhile, but it is Court Ceremonial[67] and the Way of Poetry that never lose their appeal.' He hadn't had much to do with it himself, he said, but he believed devoutly in the Way of Poetry."[68]

Lord Koresuke also said: "In the instructions Retired Emperor Fushimi left to Retired Emperor Go-Fushimi, he says that in the event of another imperial anthology, Go-Fushimi should consult with Eifukumon'in and Fuyuhira. This is something that I specifically remember Go-Shōnen'in Fuyuhira talking about," he said.

The poems of Retired Emperor Fushimi and Go-Shōnen'in are rather different.[69] That in his instructions the Retired Emperor assumes that in the end they would be in agreement is most interesting.

Someone said: "For the *Poem Contest of Different Ages*,[70] Teika was paired with Prince Motoyoshi. 'This is the first time I ever knew a poet named Prince Motoyoshi existed,' Teika quipped. Ietaka was paired with Ono no Komachi. It's understandable that Teika would not have chosen such a companion. However, since Retired Emperor Go-Toba had said many times that Prince Motoyoshi was a superb poet, it cannot have been his intention to pair Teika with an inferior match. Kintō was not included in this poem contest, because he never produced three truly excellent poems, it is said. But how could it be that someone who was looked up to as the sun or the moon throughout the Chōtoku era [995–999] and Kankō eras [1004–1011] didn't produce three poems superior enough for this contest? Later generations have been dubious."

The late master Tameyo reportedly said: "When you are going to compose a poem for a public event,[71] you should go to Hōrin[72] and compose your poem there. Young people also should go there to compose poems. The atmosphere of the place produces particularly good poems."

Tamefuji said: "Mongaku Shōnin of Takao composed five poems and brought them to Teika. 'All are most rare in conception, poems that express the essence of Buddhist teachings,' he recorded. Myōe Shōnin of Togano'o truly stands out among devotees of the Way, which is why so many of his poems were chosen for inclusion at the time of the *Shin chokusenshū.*[73] He put together a collection called *Ishinshū,* a compilation of his poems. Mongaku Shōnin's connoisseurship thus continued on."

Shingen Shōnin is reported to have said: "Mongaku Shōnin hated Saigyō. The reason was that he believed once a person had taken the tonsure he should concentrate solely on Buddhist devotions and do nothing else: anyone who lived like a dilettante, wandering around mumbling poems, was unworthy as a monk. Mongaku was always saying that he planned to crack Saigyō's skull if ever he laid eyes on him, no matter where. Mongaku's disciples lamented, thinking, 'Saigyō is a famous master; to do anything like that would cause trouble.'

"On a certain occasion, Saigyō went to a Lotus Service at Takao, and was composing poems while wandering around beneath the flowering cherry trees. Mongaku's disciples tried to keep this from their master. But after he had returned to his chambers at the conclusion of the service, someone announced that there was a visitor in the courtyard.

" 'Who is it?' he asked.

" 'Someone named Saigyō,' was the reply. 'He has come in connection with the Lotus Service and hopes to spend the night here because it's almost dark.'

" 'Well, this is my chance,' Mongaku thought, and got himself ready. Then he opened the sliding door and waited. After a short time, the servant said, 'Please, right in here,' and Saigyō came in. After hearing about him for such a long time, Mongaku now actually saw him. 'I'm most delighted that you have come to visit,' he said most cordially, and then had dinner served. The next morning, with Mongaku asking him to please come again sometime, Saigyō left. Mongaku's disciples were delighted that Saigyō had got away without incident.

" 'Seeing as how you always said that you would break his skull if you ever met him,' they said, 'haven't you gone back on your word? You were chatting with him awfully congenially.'

" 'What a bunch of dolts you are,' Mongaku said. 'He wasn't the sort to be knocked down by Mongaku; he was the sort to knock Mongaku down.' "

Someone said: "When *Senzaishū*[74] was being compiled, Saigyō was in the East Country, but he set out to return to the capital when he heard an imperial command to compile an anthology had been issued. On the way, he ran into Tōren.

"When he asked about the anthology, Tōren replied, 'It has been made public, and many of your poems are included.'

" 'And was my poem, "Snipes flying up from a marsh / on evening in autumn,"[75] among them?' Saigyō asked.

" 'I don't recall seeing it,' Tōren replied.

" 'Then there's no point in even looking at it,' Saigyō said, and headed back for the East Country."

A certain priest was up in the capital from the West Country. Spending the night at Sumiyoshi Shrine,[76] he had a dream in which lots of people, priests and laymen, men and women, high and low, were gathered in front of the shrine. There were also many of the nobility. They all seemed to be waiting for someone. After a while, a Buddhist monk in a black robe was called into the main hall, after which a grand voice intoned the poem

> Even one who claims
>   to no longer have a heart
>   feels this sad beauty:
> snipes flying up from a marsh
>   on an evening in autumn.[77]

> *kokoro naki / mi ni mo aware wa / shirarekeri*
> *shigi tatsu sawa no / aki no yūgure*

So I was told.

Kunifuyu, Chief Priest of Sumiyoshi Shrine, said this: "Many poets have become patrons of my shrine. Michitsune, Governor of Izumi Province, was seen by people, in demon form, with paper and brush in hand, sitting on the platform in the northwest corner of the guard's enclosure, facing west." So the story goes.

Kunisuke Kaminushi built a shrine beside Shiragi Temple,[78] where he is worshipped. He was called Imanushinokami. He is one of the masters of this Way of recent years.

> What a happy thought—
> that the fence around my shrine
>   is what protects
> the god who guards the Way
>   of Our Many Islands.[79]

> *shikishima no / michi mamorikeru / kami o shi mo*
> *waga kamigaki to / omou ureshisa*

Exactly the way he must have felt, I should think. He was allowed to attend banquets, and at the time of the *Shin gosenshū*,[80] seventeen of his poems—the same number as for Hidetō—were included. He was peerless in both practice and reputation. However, he developed an obsession with the fact that Ietaka had composed 60,000 poems. Although he had already proved himself with many fine poems, now he wrote a thousand poems each month. From that time on, his poems lost their elegance, because so many were marred by frightful images. The current master, Tamesada, said that one should take precautions against such things. The Tō Lay Monk Yukiuji also composed a hundred poems every month, and none of them were of the sort to be included in an imperial anthology, he said.

The late master Tameyo said: "When you are a novice, you should compose love poems all the time. Then you will gain experience in both conception and diction."

The late master Tameyo also said: "According to Tameie, cutting just one line from an old poem and composing a poem with that as a topic is good practice for novices. Because you must arrange things in such a way as to not alter the words of the original poem, your command of style will improve and your diction will be elegant."

Imperial anthologies have other names. *Goshūishū*,[81] for instance, is called the *Horse Mackerel Collection*—a name probably given because Tsumori Kunimoto brought a gift of horse mackerel to the compiler as an appeal and got a lot of his poems included.[82] *Kinyōshū*[83] is called *Hijitsuki Aruji*, which probably means "Inferior Anthology."[84] *Shin chokusenshū* is called *Uji River Collection* because there are so many poems by warriors in it.[85] *Shoku shūishū*[86] is called *Cormorant Boat Collection* because it includes so many poems about watch fires.[87] Some slanderers call the *Shin gosenshū* the *Tsumori Collection*, perhaps because it includes many poems by officials of Sumiyoshi Shrine.[88] These days, too, there are those who lampoon imperial collections, but I guess none of them has the imagination to come up with a name.

When the late master Tameyo had received the command for the *Shoku senzaishū*[89] and was selecting poems, sometimes people who really were not poets would come calling. "Yes, it's an imperial anthology, with poems by the nobility," he would say, "but by all means submit your own." Tamefuji and some other disciples thought that since an imperial anthology was so important for the Way, only truly superb poems should be chosen; they feared that asking people who didn't compose poems to submit work would lead to criticism and was simply improper. The next time Tameyo met with them, having heard about this grumbling, he said: "*Uta* is a practice of this country. Who born into this country doesn't compose poems?[90] There are those who undertake practice and gain reputation in the world; there are those who compose alone, just to cultivate their hearts. In old anthologies there are excellent poems that were submitted by people who were not poets—the poem of the eight-year-old in the *Gosenshū,* for example.[91] Having received an imperial command to compile an anthology, I am searching for good poems. As I do so, it may be that someone who is not a poet has composed a superb poem. How could I fail to announce my project broadly?" he said. They all thought this was an interesting reply.

Nōyo was a poet especially favored by the late master Tameyo. He was a beloved disciple of the late Bishop of Karyūji. His poem

> Learn from the heart
>   of one who knows about grieving,
> you cuckoo calling—
> from one who in sorrow's depths
>   still weeps only softly.

wabibito no / kokoro ni narae / hototogisu /
uki ni zo yasuku / ne wa nakarekeru

was put into *Shin gosenshū* as an anonymous poem;[92] and
when Retired Emperor Go-Nijō was putting poems from that
anthology on screens, I understand that he included this one.

The late master thought highly of the following poems
and told people about them:

> At Meeting Hill
>   the moonlight must not have stopped
>   to spend the night:
> for there it was in the west
>   as we passed the gate next morn.

ausaka ya / tsui ni tomaranu / tsukikage o /
seki no to akete / nishi ni miru kana

> Let's head off now
>   toward the house that must be there
>   where a dog is barking—
> and ask the man he's barking at
>   for a place to spend the night.

sato no inu no / koe suru kata o / shirube nite /
togamuru hito ni / yado ya karamashi

"Not the sort of thing one would recommend as a model of
style," I thought, and was ill at ease about it.

Then, when I was living in the Eastern Hills near Sō-
rinji, Nōyo came to visit me. "While I have known of you
for some time," he said, "I have never been able to meet you
at poetry gatherings. I'm going down to Tsukushi soon and

may never be in the capital again, so I have come to see you—please forgive the impertinence." He was not at all accomplished in the Way, he said; he had never really undergone training in composition, nor did he claim any inborn talent for composing poems. "I really don't understand myself why the master Tameyo has such kind things to say about me. It must be a bond from a former existence," he said.

I chatted with him for a while, and it was clear that he hadn't done much reading. "The sort of person the world calls a connoisseur," I thought to myself.

According to Tameuji, Lord Kaneuji was capable both in practice and in composition. In a letter sent to someone, he also said that Kaneuji was not inferior to secretaries in the ministries in his knowledge of things related to the compilation of imperial anthologies. At the time of the *Shoku shūishū*,[93] he was one of the fellows in the Poetry Bureau, but he died before the compilation was completed. Among his poems was this one:

> Descending ever—
> like the plank bridge decaying
>   at Obatada—
> so are the tears of lovers
>   who are never able to meet.[94]

> *obatada no / itada no hashi to / koboruru wa*
> *wataranu naka no / namida narikeri*

which he had been told would be put in the anthology. Dharma Eye Keiyū, however, had reservations. That night, in a dream, Keiyū met Kaneuji on the veranda in one corner of the entry gate to the Reizei mansion. Kaneuji gripped him around the waist and said, "A poet is still concerned after he has passed on." "It seemed he was resentful that Keiyū had voiced reservations about including the poem," he thought. Later, Keiyū developed an infirmity in his back and was never free of it. What fearsome dedication! And Kaneuji's son, Dharma Sign Chōshun, was not inferior in his dedication to the Way. He said, "Someday I will become a baby snake or a baby mouse in the Poetry Bureau offices; so if you see something of that sort, please refrain from harming it." At the time of *Shoku goshūiūshū*,[95] after he had died, a baby snake was seen among the books there, and someone was quick to say that it must be Chōshun. In particular, this put a scare into Dharma Sign Jisshō.

Lord Takanori lacked ability when he was young,[96] so he went to Sumiyoshi and Tamatsushima[97] and prayed devoutly. Perhaps for that reason, lately his approach has gained sway, and he has developed a reputation.[98] His poetry contest judgments appear to remind people of those of old. Last year he came to a poetry meeting at the house of Master Tamesada. People felt that his manner of reading[99] and handling of poems[100] were worthy of praise.

The late master Tameyo also felt that the style of Kujō of the Second Rank in the lector's seat was not at all similar to those of Koretsugu and Sanetō.

Arifusa said: "Once Tameie held a thousand-verse *renga* sequence at his Chū'in Mansion in Saga, with the same first verse for all ten hundred–verse sequences. The verse that he used as his first verse he recorded for later generations:

A brocade, perhaps—
such is the look of Saga
in the autumn time.

nishiki ka to / aki wa sagano no / miyuru kana

One wonders why can't there be *hokku* like this today.

On the last day of the Ninth Month, Lay-Monk Nobuzane invited a group of literati to come with him to the home of Ryūshin Shōnin in Fukakusa, where they composed linked verse. Tameie's *hokku* was

> Today, already
> here we are at the very end
> of autumn.

> *kefu wa haya / aki no kagiri ni / narinikeri*

That night they spent composing linked verse, and were preparing to leave in the morning when Ryūshin said, "Today is the first day of winter. How about it? Why don't we do it." So they composed a *renga* again. Since none of those assembled knew the rules very well, Tameie wrote the *hokku* again:

> Today, already
> here we are at the beginning
> of winter.

> *kesa wa haya / fuyu no hajime ni / narinikeri*

A *hokku* serves just to begin the banquet, and needn't always aim for real feeling.[101]

One autumn, Tameuji was composing *renga* at the temple of Ryūshin Shōnin in Fukakusa. He heard that Mushō was there, summoned him, and had him compose a *hokku:*

> Cry out, then, cry—
> you crickets in the heavy dew
> of Fukakusa.[102]

> *nake ya nake / tsuyu fukakusa no / kirigirisu*

Everyone was very impressed. Why is it that those crowds meeting beneath the blossoms these days can't come up with something like this? I wonder.

Tamefuji said: "Among the nonprofessional poets of our day are Tominokōji Sanenori and Nakamikado Tsunetsugu, both major counselors. Tominokōji's poems are not as lofty in conception as those of his father, Kin'o, but he is a poet who puts great effort into every poem and never comes up short. As for Nakamikado, he became a disciple of the Tameuji back in the days when he was serving as Clearance Officer[103] and visited all the time. His poems are always seemly, and he keeps careful records. His style to this day appears to be straightforward and correct.

"There is something of interest and attractive in each of Tominokōji's poems. Yet, in choosing poems to put in an imperial anthology, none of his is acceptable. In a poetry session, Nakamikado seems much less able, but when it comes to choosing poems for an imperial anthology, many of his are acceptable."

The current master, Tamesada, says the same thing.

Tamefuji said this: "Teika always said, 'My late father was a beautiful poet; as for me, I'm just a versifier.[104] I set out to compose poems like those of my father, but I wasn't up to it, so I stopped trying.

"'Yet, both Tōken and Seikaku,[105] however different in style, gained praised as preachers; and in the same way, there seem to be those for whom my poems stand out, even though they are different in style from those of my late father.'"

Tamefuji also said that Urabe Nakasuke had written about this matter in the same way.

Tamefuji said this: "In a letter written to Reverend Jichin, Teika said, 'Your poems and those of my late father are by beautiful poets. Teika is a versifier who just constructs poems using the power of learning. All under heaven who construct poems are my disciples.'"

Once when Tamefuji visited Retired Emperor Go-Uda, His Majesty asked him about proper poetic style. Tamefuji said: "There's really not that much to poetry. Take as your model this poem by the wife of the Uzumasa Monk:[106]

WRITTEN AT THE END OF THE YEAR,
WHEN SHE WAS SUFFERING FROM
WORLDLY TROUBLES

As I take apart
    the causes of my sadness
        on this winter night,
the only thing unfrozen still
    is the current of my tears.

*mi no usa o / omoishitokeba / fuyu no yo mo
todokoranu wa / namida narikeri*

His closest attendants said that Go-Uda remained impressed ever after that Tameuji had said this was the foundation of poetry. "The author was not an especially accomplished poet, but the poem achieves an intensity of feeling, and its words come together most naturally, producing a poem truly praiseworthy in effect," he thought.

Once Tameie was passing by the house of Shinkan and saw a carriage decorated with a sparrow design parked there. When he had a servant go and ask whose carriage it was, he was informed that it was the carriage of the Governor of Hyūga (Lord Kaneuji). This made Tameie so furious that after returning home, he went directly to the Poetry Bureau and cut from the imperial anthology the three poems by Kaneuji that had been selected for inclusion.[107]

Chōshun and Junkyō took the tonsure and lived in the Pine Shade Villa at Kajūji. Chōshun left and became a Confucian scholar in the area around Shōren'in, while Junkyō (Shun'e) went down to the East Country and made a name for himself as a ying-yang master—his original field. In the beginning, Chōshun went to the East Country as a monk and appeared now and again at Ōmidō, going by the sobriquet Kan'e. The judgment of people in poetry gatherings here and there was that his poems were too restrained.[108] This is why poems in the restrained style are in the East Country referred to as in the manner of Lord Kan.[109]

Tamefuji said: "When Consultant Toshikoto became a courtier, Tamekane nominated him to serve as lector. In reading the title 'Minister of the Left,' he didn't know that it was to be pronounced *hidan no ōimochigimi*.[110] Tamekane hadn't taught him this; perhaps he didn't know it himself. Most amusing."[111]

One should show formal poems to other people, and have poems submitted for public occasions revised. For *The Hundred Poem Sequence of the Kagen Era*,[112] Jō'i wrote this poem:

> All along the road
>   peasants are loaded with pine boughs
>   to place at the gate—
> looking to be in a hurry
>   to wait for the year's end.[113]

michinobe ni / shizu ga kadomatsu / ninaimote
isogu to miyuru / toshi no kure kana

This poem was also included in *The Hundred Poem Sequence of the Bunpō Era*.[114] This is a mistake of old age for a man long dedicated to the Way. It happened because he didn't even show the poem to other disciples of the house.

To write down drafts for a round of poems[115] at a poetic gathering and show them to people, or copy down a poem and put it in your breast pocket so that you can record it later—such things were never done by the adepts of the past. It is only recently that this has gone on. There are even cases when a person hands out paper to each person after topics have been passed out, and then collects them from everyone—a truly unsightly practice. To carry one's poem around as if it's something outstanding makes one look silly. It is simply inappropriate to be showing a poem composed extemporaneously to people at a gathering, soliciting corrections, and so on. The way people of late stick their heads together to arrive at judgments is most unseemly.

Jō'i said: "Because imperial anthologies are used to flatter those of high rank and to grant favor to their lackeys, true skill in composition, elegant taste, and practice have become of secondary importance—with the result that distinctions between the good and the bad in the Way cannot easily emerge. The intent over the years was to solicit preliminary collections[116] for consideration, and then make choices based on the relative value of the poems; but since people are just as sensitive about preliminary collections, the plans come to nothing."

Once when Tamefuji had an audience with the Go-Saionji Lay-Monk Chancellor Sanekane, he was asked which would be more beneficial for a beginning poet—to mark many poems as excellent, or only a few?[117] Someone said that ever after, Sanekane said how impressed he was that Tamefuji said it would be more beneficial to mark only a few.

Lord Reizei Tamehide said: "At the time *Fūgashū*[118] was being compiled, I went to the Hagiwara Palace and often talked with Retired Emperor Hanazono. 'Of the poems I know by Lord Tamekane,' he said, 'I would take this one as the model:

Even the bird calls
    ring serene in the mountains
        as morning opens;
and the color of the haze
    has the look of spring.[119]

*tori no ne mo / nodokeki yama no / asaake ni
kasumi no iro mo / harumekinikeri*

Over the years, I have asked my elders if, looking at old texts, one should not conclude that it is poems of lofty and beautiful configuration[120] we should regard as supreme. The "highest of the highest rank" among the nine grades is given to poems of lofty conception, elegant diction, and overtones of intense feeling, it is said.[121] And Tadamine and Michinari give first place among their ten styles to those in the archaic, mysterious, gentle styles, and the style of overtones.[122] According to the writings of Teika, these poems by Minamoto no Shunrai should serve as models for public poems, and poems of high formality:

The cherry blossoms
    seem now to be all in bloom.
Off in the distance,
against clouds in the heavens—
the white threads of a waterfall.[123]

*sakurabana / sakinikerashi na / hisakata no
kumoi ni miyuru / taki no shiraito*

In the swift stream
    coursing by like the mighty men
        of Uji River,

the waves pass over boulders—
no more numerous than your years.[124]

mononofu no / yasoujikawa no / hayaki se ni
iwakosu nami wa / chiyo no kazu ka mo

Among recent poets, the one to look up to is Tameie. Ta-
mekane and Tamehide descend from him, and have split off
into varying styles; but who would not look up to their fore-
bear? Even when he was very ill, in the eleventh year of the
Bun'ei era [1274], and put together his best poems of that
period into a hundred-poem contest, with Kaneuji as his
scribe, the poems were not anything special in terms of
style—just mellifluous and full of feeling.

Since the time of Shunzei, it is the poems the masters chose
from among their own poems for inclusion in imperial an-
thologies and those of their heirs that they first put into im-
perial anthologies that represent their truest intentions. In
this connection: *Senzaishū* still retains some features of the
style of mid-antiquity[125] and does not always measure up.
Likewise, *Shin kokinshū* is a product of the designs of its
various compilers and the Retired Emperor [Go-Toba] and
contains things that were not to the liking of Teika.[126] The
eleven poems of the compiler and six poems of his heir in
Shin chokusenshū; the eleven poems of the compiler and six
poems of his heir in *Shoku gosenshū*; the eleven poems of the
compiler and six poems of his heir in *Shoku shūishū*—these
are the poems that one should regard as the most fundamen-
tal models of style.[127]

   In recent times, poetry has divided into many currents,
with cronies at poetic gatherings always ready with their vari-
ous opinions, throwing my old heart into confusion and leav-
ing me looking for the one path I first heard of long ago.
Being somewhat at a loss about how to proceed from now
on, I put these notes together, beginning with the nine grades

and the ten styles[128] and continuing on to poems favored by particular authors. I have put them all in one box and given them the name "From a Frog at the Bottom of a Well."

NOTES

1. *Yūgen.* A prominent critical term of praise, especially associated with the poetry and criticism of Fujiwara no Shunzei and his generation, indicating the suggestion of profound meaning beneath the surface.

2. *Giri fukaku shite.* A descriptive phrase probably related to Teika's own characterization of his work as that of a versifier who relies on learning rather than profound spiritual understanding. See pp. 207–208.

3. This is the last poem of *Kagetsu hyakushu,* 1190. See Kubota Jun, ed., *Yakuchū Fujiwara no Teika zenkashū,* vol. 1 (Tokyo: Kawade Shobō, 1985), p. 107.

4. The poem appears in round 38 of *Teika-kyō hyakuban jika-awase.* See Higuchi Yoshimaro et al., *Chūsei wakashū, Kamakura hen,* vol. 46 of *Shin Nihon koten bungaku taikei* (Tokyo: Iwanami Shoten, 1991), p. 133.

5. Probably what offended Tameie was the repetition of "moon" in the phrase *nagatsuki no / tsuki no ariake* (In the moonlight / of the dawn moon of the Long Month).

6. Kubota Jun points out that in his later years Teika himself was rather critical of such syntactic constructions (*Yakuchū Fujiwara no Teika zenkashū,* vol. 1, p. 107).

7. *Collection of Jeweled Leaves,* 1313. Fourteenth of the imperial anthologies, compiled by the order of Jimyō'in Emperor Fushimi by Kyōgoku Tamekane, both of whom were rivals of the Nijō house. Standard texts of all the imperial anthologies are available in *Shinpen Kokka taikan,* vol. 1 (Tokyo: Kadokawa Shoten, 1983).

8. Tonna is correct. The poem does not appear in *Gyokuyōshū.*

9. The poem in question is number 2603 in Teika's personal anthology, *Shūi gusō.* The incident related here took place in

1220. Go-Toba was evidently offended because Teika's poem—which is doubtless a personal lament—seemed to allude to a poem by Sugawara no Michizane, who was sent into exile after being falsely accused by wicked ministers of the sovereign. Whether Teika intended such a comparison is unknown, but Teika was banned from court for a time. For a complete account, see Kubota Jun, *Fujiwara Teika: Ran ni hana ari* (Tokyo: Shueisha, 1984), pp. 214–218.

10. This probably is a reference to an incident recorded in Go-Toba's own *Go-Toba' in go-kuden.* See Robert H. Brower, "Ex-Emperor Go-Toba's Secret Teachings," *Harvard Journal of Asiatic Studies* 32 (1972): 39–40.

11. This is poem number 1776 in Ietaka's personal anthology, *Minishū.* See *Shinpen Kokka taikan,* vol. 3 (Tokyo: Kadokawa Shoten, 1990).

12. *New Imperial Collection,* 1234. Ninth of the imperial anthologies, compiled by Fujiwara no Teika.

13. *Hanayaka.*

14. *Shinchokusenshū* 40.

15. *Shoku goshūishū* 41, by Fujiwara no Tameuji. The headnote there reads: "On 'A Spring View of an Inlet,' written in the second year of the Kenchō era for a contest involving Chinese and Japanese poems."

16. A contest held in 1250.

17. *Kamuyakami no tatekami.* Sasaki Takahiro et al. note that although in the Heian period this term referred to the fine papers produced for official documents at court, by the early Kamakura period the word indicated darker, recycled paper (*Karon kagaku shūsei,* vol. 10 [Tokyo: Miyai Shoten, 1999], p. 443, n. 52).

18. A different version of this story appears in *Shōtetsu monogatari.* See Robert H. Brower and Steven D. Carter, *Conversations with Shōtetsu* (Ann Arbor: Center for Japanese Studies, University of Michigan, 1992), p. 103.

19. *Tanzaku.* A long sheet of stiff paper on which poems were recorded.

20. *Shinchokusenshū* 565.

21. *Sōshi*. Here, probably a reference to books of poetry.

22. "Blue clouds" probably means something like "clouds in the blue sky"—that is, the natural world itself rather than old poems.

23. *Later Collection Continued,* 1251. Tenth of the imperial anthologies, compiled by Fujiwara no Tameie.

24. Teachers "marked" poems submitted by students that they judged to be outstanding, usually with a diagonal brushstroke just above the poem.

25. The name of Tameie's house in Saga, also pronounced Nakano'in.

26. *Shin chokusenshū* 794.

27. *Collection of Ancient and Modern Times,* 905. First of the imperially commissioned anthologies of court poetry.

28. An area in modern Ōtsu City. The place of Ben no Naishi's actual retirement was, in fact, nearer Yokawa.

29. Ancient Chinese mythology had it that each year on the seventh day of the Seventh Month, the Herd Boy (Altair) and the Weaver Maiden (Vega)—kept apart by their parents—met for just one night across the bridge provided by the Milky Way. Poets met on that month to write poems honoring the couple.

30. *Shin shūishū* 1587.

31. *Kokin no setsu*. A reference to the coveted "secret teachings" of the house concerning *Kokinshū* and other early poetic texts. Tameyo received his grandfather's secret teachings in Saga when he was fifteen years old.

32. According to Tō no Tsuneyori, a disciple of Tonna's descendant Gyōkō, Tonna uttered this sentence as his last words. See *Tōyashū kikigaki,* in *Nihon kagaku taikei,* vol. 5. (Tokyo: Kazama Shobō, 1957), p. 377.

33. *Collection of Ancient and Modern Times Continued,* 1265. Eleventh of the imperial anthologies, compiled by Fujiwara no Tameie and others.

34. In fact, twenty-five of her poems appear in imperial anthologies, including those compiled after her death.

35. *Wakan kensakushū*. A mid–Kamakura period anthology that

brings together works by poets famous for both their Japanese and their Chinese poems. Imadegawa'in Konoe is the only woman represented in the collection. See *Shinpen Kokka taikan,* vol. 6 (Tokyo: Kadodawa Shoten, 1985).

36. The most widely read of all the Mahayana sutras.

37. *Shōbugasane.* Ladies arranged their robes to create a "layered effect" of colors. This one involved a combination of varying shades of blue-green and pink.

38. The last phrase, an obscure passage, translates: *kuruma yori mo ori mo sede, makariidete haberishi.* I follow Sasaki in favoring *ori mo sede* over the *orite* of the *Nihon kagaki taikei* text (*Karon kagaku shūsei,* vol. 10, pp. 312, 447, n. 92).

39. *Jin no za.* Originally, a guard's chamber, but generally used for formal meetings of courtiers.

40. The poet Shinkei relates a story about Shunzei with a similar message. See *Sasamegoto,* in *Rengaronshū,* vol. 50 of *Nihon koten bungaku taikei* (Tokyo: Iwanami Shoten, 1961), p. 146.

41. A prominent temple that had originated as a noble residence.

42. *Uta no ma.*

43. The main hall of an aristocrat's dwelling.

44. *Roppyaku-ban uta-awase,* organized by Minister of the Left Fujiwara no Yoshitsune in 1192/1193.

45. *Tokko,* a short, double-pointed steel lance used in various esoteric Buddhist rituals; *kamakubi,* a rod with a crooked, cobra-shaped headpiece.

46. *Kakinomoto* and *kurinomoto.*

47. *Ushin,* or poems displaying aristocratic diction and taste; *mushin,* or humorous or unorthodox poems.

48. Source unknown.

49. Source unknown.

50. Source unknown.

51. *Ensho jisshu uta-awase,* more generally known as *Entō on-uta-awase.* A mock contest commissioned by Retired Emperor Go-Toba after his exile to Oki Island. In 1236, the Retired Emperor commissioned Fujiwara no Ietaka to solicit poems from fifteen poets for the contest, each writing ten poems on prescribed topics.

52. Poem number 50 in the contest, from round 25.

53. *Shin kokinshū* 114, a famous poem by Fujiwara no Shunzei.

54. It was completed in 1205, with revisions thereafter.

55. Fujiwara no Hidetō, or Hideyoshi.

56. Twelve of his poems were included in the anthology.

57. *Hōji hyakushu.* A set of sequences solicited from forty poets by Retired Emperor Go-Saga in 1248.

58. In his later years, Tomoie sided with Shinkan and others against Teika's son and heir, Tameie.

59. *Shoku gosenshū* 1118. The headnote there reads: "On 'The Moon at an Old Temple.'" The place name Takano refers to Mount Kōya, site of the most important of the Shingon monasteries, where the light of Buddhist law, symbolized by the moonlight, shines amid the darkness of the world.

60. *Nusa.*

61. "Initiating verse," a term referring to the first verse of a linked verse sequence.

62. The author of the first verse of a sequence was required to work into the syntax of his poem an answer to a kind of riddle: "*What* path?"→ a *mountain* path.

63. Source unknown.

64. *Mōshitsugi.*

65. This anecdote does not appear in extant versions of *Ben no Naishi nikki.*

66. *Shodō.* No doubt referring mostly to such courtly arts as practicing calligraphy and playing musical instruments.

67. *Jomoku no koto.* The study of procedures, customs, and regulations associated with various court offices.

68. In fact, Enkō'in—Takatsukasa Mototada—was quite active in poetic circles. More than eighty of his poems appear in imperial anthologies.

69. Fuyuhira is generally considered to have been an adherent of Nijō poetics rather than of the Kyōgoku school of Fushimi.

70. *Jidai fudō uta-awase.* A 150-round contest concocted by Retired Emperor Go-Toba in the mid-1230s that pitted poets from the early ages (until the time of *Shūishū*) against poets from later ages in a mock competition format.

71. *Hare no uta.* A formal poem for a contest or public gathering.

72. An area to the west of the capital, in Saga.

73. Five of his poems appear in the anthology.

74. *Collection of a Thousand Years,* 1188. Seventh of the imperial anthologies, compiled by Fujiwara no Shunzei.

75. One of Saigyō's most famous poems, it was later included in *Shin kokinshū* as number 3620.

76. Located in Settsu Province, Sakai. It is a shrine to Sumiyoshi Myōjin, a patron god of poets.

77. *Shin kokinshū* 362.

78. I am following Sasaki in favoring Shiragidera over Jingoji (*Karon kagaku shūsei,* vol. 10, p. 456, no. 185). The former refers to a temple within the Sumiyoshi Shrine complex.

79. *Shin gosenshū* 742.

80. *New Later Collection,* 1303. Thirteenth of the imperial anthologies, compiled by Nijō Tameyo and members of the Tsumori family.

81. *Later Collection of Gleanings,* 1086. Fourth of the imperial anthologies, compiled by Fujiwara no Michitoshi.

82. Three of his poems were included, more than was to be expected for one of his rank and stature.

83. *Collection of Golden Leaves,* 1126. Fifth of the imperial anthologies, compiled by Minamoto no Shunrai.

84. The meaning of the title is unclear. See Fujioka Tadaharu, ed., *Fukurō zōshi,* vol. 29 of *Shin Nihon koten bungaku taikei* (Tokyo: Iwanami Shoten, 1995). It was evidently Fujiwara no Moritsune who gave it the name. The title *Kin'yōshū* (Collection of golden leaves) was considered to have unlucky connotations because "golden leaves" were reported to have fallen at the time of the Buddha's death.

85. The connection of the Uji River and warriors goes back to a famous poem attributed to Kakinomoto no Hitomaro (*Man'yōshū* 266), in which the river is referred to as "the river of the emperor's mighty men."

86. *Collection of Gleanings Continued,* 1278. Twelfth of the imperial anthologies, compiled by Fujiwara no Tameuji.

87. *Kagari.* Such fires were used to attract fish at night by cormorant fishermen. However, the title probably is a veiled reference to the prominence of poems by military men—who stood watch around "watch fires"—in the anthology.

88. The anthology contains many poems by Nijō Tamyo's in-laws of the Tsumori family, who held the hereditary headship of Sumiyoshi Shrine.

89. *Collection of a Thousand Years Continued,* 1320. Fifteenth of the imperial anthologies, compiled by Fujiwara no Tameyo.

90. An allusion to the famous *Kokinshū* preface: "The song of the warbler among the blossoms, the voice of the frog dwelling in the water—these teach us that every living creature sings." See Helen Craig McCullough, *Kokin Wakashū: The First Imperial Anthology of Japanese Poetry* (Stanford, Calif.: Stanford University Press, 1985), p. 3.

91. The headnote to *Gosenshū* 461 reads: "Sent when her parent had gone away and was late coming back (written by a girl of eight).”

92. *Shin gosenshū* 1277.

93. *Collection of Gleanings Continued,* 1278.

94. The poem eventually was included in the last imperial anthology, *Shin shokukokinshū,* as number 1143.

95. *Later Collection of Gleanings Continued,* 1325. Sixteenth of the imperial anthologies, compiled by Nijō Tamefuji and Nijō Tamesada.

96. Inoue Muneo notes that when encouraged to have Takanori serve as lector for a poetic event in 1289, the young man's father demurred because his son was not ready for such a task (*Chūsei kadan shi no kenkyū, Nanbokuchō hen* [Tokyo: Meiji Shoin, 1987], p. 20). Later, Takanori became one of the major court poets in the Kyōgoku style.

97. Shintō shrines whose deities were sacred to Japanese poets.

98. The sentence translates: *saru yue ni ya, chikagoro wa michi mo saru tei ni narite hito mo shiriki.* I have interpreted *michi mo saru tei ni narite* to mean that of late, the Kyōgoku style has gained in popularly again, with the advent of Reizei Tamehide at court. An alternative interpretation would be: "Per-

haps for that reason, lately he has developed a worthy style, and gained a reputation."

99. *Hikō no tei.* A reference to his way of reading poems aloud as lector at a poetry meeting.

100. *Utamotenashi.* A vague expression that could refer to his "handling" of poetic composition but also to his "handling" of the etiquette involved in producing poems in a formal setting.

101. In his *Azuma mondō,* the *renga* poet Sōgi attributes these verses, in slightly altered form, to Tameie's consort, the nun Abutsu. See *Rengaronshū haironshū,* vol. 66 of *Nihon koten bungaku taikei* (Tokyo: Iwanami Shoten, 1961), p. 218.

102. An allusion to *Goshūishū* 273, a famous *uta* by Sone no Yoshitada.

103. *Kageyushi.* The officer responsible for arranging for smooth transitions of power between retiring and newly appointed provincial governors.

104. The contrast being made here is between *utayomi,* a term of praise that Teika evidently reserved for his father and Jichin, and *utazukuri,* which he uses for himself.

105. Chōken and Seikaku were also father and son and yet had different styles of preaching.

106. In *Kin'yōshū,* where it appears as number 584, the poem is labeled "anonymous." In *Mumyōshō,* the poem is attributed to a court lady identified as the wife of the Awaji Ajari of Ninnaji. See *Nihon koten bungaku taikei,* vol. 65 (Tokyo: Iwanami Shoten, 1961), p. 70. The poem is given as an example of a poem by an untrained person under the influence of strong emotion.

107. Shinkan was Tameie's chief rival. The imperial anthology alluded to in the anecdote is probably *Shoku kokinshū,* which was compiled by Tameie, Shinkan, and a number of other poets. Only one of Kaneuji's poems was included in the final text.

108. *Heikai.*

109. An abbreviated form of Kan'e.

110. *Hidan* is a contracted form of *hidari* (left).

111. Knowledge of such matters was expected of the heirs of poetic houses, such as the Kyōgoku. For Tamekane not to have taught his heir about such things was a reflection of his lack of "seriousness" as a poet in the minds of his opponents of the Nijō camp.

112. *Kagen hyakushu,* 1303. The poem does not in fact appear in this anthology.

113. *Bunpō hyakushu* 3066, another version of the poem, reads slightly differently: "Ready to celebrate, people are loaded with pine boughs . . . (*iwau beki / tami no kado matsu*). A pine bough was placed at the corner of the gate as a prayer for prosperity in the new year.

114. *Bunpō hyakushu,* 1320.

115. *Tsugiuta.* A round of poems—a hundred, in many cases—generally composed extemporaneously.

116. *Uchigiki.* A term for various "personal collections" put together with the idea of providing raw material for later imperial anthologies.

117. It was the custom for students of masters such as Tamefuji to present their poems for "marking," which teachers usually did with a diagonal brushstroke.

118. *Collection of Elegance,* 1346. Seventeenth of the imperial anthologies, compiled by Retired Emperor Kōgon and Retired Emperor Hanazono.

119. *Gyokuyōshū* 9.

120. *Takaku, uruwashiki sugata.* Poems of lofty diction and conventionally beautiful form.

121. A reference to the *Waka kuhon* of Fujiwara no Kintō. Kintō divides his eighteen exemplary poems into nine grades, and classifies them into highest, middle, and lowest grades within each category. See *Waka kuhon,* in *Karonshū, nōgakuronshū,* vol. 65 of *Nihon koten bungaku taikei* (Tokyo: Iwanami Shoten, 1961), p. 32.

122. *Tadamine jittei* is the title of a list of fifty exemplary poems in ten categories attributed to the tenth-century poet Mibu no Tadamine, although almost certainly by a later hand and from a later date. *Michinari jittei* is a later text that derives

directly from *Tadamine jittei,* attributed to Minamoto no Michinari. For a text of *Tadamine jittei,* see *Nihon kagaku taikei,* vol. 1 (Tokyo: Kazama Shoin, 1957). The first four categories in *Tadamine jittei* are indeed those Tonna lists: the *koka tei,* the *shinmyō tei,* the *sunao naru tei,* and the *yojō tei.*

123. The first two lines in the original (*Kinyōshū* 50) actually read: *yamazakura / sakisomeshi yori* (since first blossoming / of the mountain cherry trees).

124. A congratulatory poem written in praise of Fujiwara no Morozane for *The Kaya no In Poetry Contest* of 1094 (*Senzaishū* 615). The first line of the poem actually reads: *ochitagitsu* (cascading rapids), rather than *mononofu no* (like the mighty men).

125. *Chūko no fū.* For Tonna, probably a reference to the days before the Mikohidari lineage of Shunzei had established itself as preeminent at court.

126. Eleven compilers were first appointed to put together this anthology, with three more added later, plus the librarian for the project, Minamoto no Ienaga.

127. These three imperial anthologies were assembled by compilers working alone—Teika, Tameie, and Tameuji. The numbers given here—eleven poems for each compiler, six for their heirs—are incorrect. Earlier in *Seiashō,* however, Tonna notes that Shunzei first chose eleven of his poems for inclusion and was then asked by the emperor to include more. This no doubt became a tradition. See *Nihon kagaku taikei,* vol. 5 (Tokyo: Kazama Shobō, 1957), pp. 26–28.

128. See note 122.

Glossary of Important Names and Places

AKAI PRINCE (precise dates unknown)   Also known by his Buddhist name, Dōshō. Son of Emperor Kameyama. Major Archbishop and chief priest of Daigoji and Sanbō'in cloister (Poem 63)

AKIIE   *See* Rokujō Akiie

ASHIKAGA TADAYOSHI (1306–1352)   Younger brother of Shogun Ashikaga Takauji (Poem 70)

ASHIKAGA TAKAUJI (1305–1358)   First of the Ashikaga shoguns. Tutored in poetry by Nijō Tamesada. Patron of the Nijō house, Tonna, and other Nijō poets (Poems 18, 92, 103)

ASHIKAGA YOSHIAKIRA (1330–1367)   Son of Shogun Takauji and second of the Ashikaga shoguns. Patron of the Nijō house, the Reizei house, Tonna, and other Nijō poets (Poems 95, 111, 123)

ASUKAI NORISADA (1210–1266)   Son and heir of Asukai Masatsune. Married his daughter to Fujiwara no Tameuji of the Mikohidari house and became a strong adherent of Nijō poetics

AUGI   A place north of Sakamoto

AUSAKA   Site of an important barrier in Ōmi Province, on the road leading east

AZUMA   *See* East Country

BEN NO NAISHI (precise dates unknown)   Daughter of Fujiwara no Nobuzane. Lady-in-waiting to Emperor Go-Fukakusa and author of a famous diary, *Ben no Naishi nikki*

BISHOP OF KŌRYŪJI (1249–1304)   Former Archbishop Shūyo

BISHOP SOMETHING-OR-OTHER   Identity unknown

BŌJŌ TOSHIZANE (1296–1350)   Governor General of Dazaifu

COMMANDER OF THE LEFT GUARDS   *See* Ashikaga Tadayoshi

CHAMBERLAIN-MIDDLE COUNSELOR   *See* Nijō Tameakira

CHŌKEN (precise dates unknown)   Son of Fujiwara no Michinori, of the Okazaki sub-lineage. Tendai monk known for his ability as a preacher

CHŌSHUN HŌ'IN (d. 1325?)   Also known as Kan'e. Son of Minamoto no Kaneuji. Librarian in the Poetry Bureau during the compilation of *Shin gosenshū* and *Shoku senzaishū*

CONSULTANT TOSHIKOTO   *See* Fujiwara no Toshikoto

CHŪ'IN   *See* Nakano'in

DANSHŌ PRINCE   *See* Kunimi Shinnō and Tadafusa (Poems 96, 110)

DAUGHTER OF TAIRA NO CHIKAKIYO (precise dates unknown)   Daughter of the warrior Nii no Kishirō Taira no Chikakiyo, mentioned in *Heike monogatari*. Court lady and poet

DHARMA EYE KEIYŪ   *See* Keiyū Hōgan

DHARMA EYE KEN'YŌ   *See* Ken'yo

DHARMA EYE TAIKAKU   *See* Taikaku

DHARMA SIGN CHŌSHUN   *See* Chōshun Hō'in

DHARMA SIGN JŌBEN   *See* Joben Ho'in

DHARMA SIGN KEIUN   *See* Keiun Hō'in.

EAST COUNTRY   General name given to the provinces around modern-day Tokyo

EASTERN HILLS   Mountains running along the eastern border of the Kyōto basin. Site of many temples, shrines, and villas during Tonna's day

EASY RIVER   *See* Yasukawa

EIFUKUMON'IN (1271–1342)   Consort of Emperor Fushimi. Major poet of the Kyōgoku school

ENKŌ'IN   *See* Takatsukasa Mototada

ENKŪ (d. 1284)   Abbot of Ōjō'in cloister, a Pure Land temple

EVERGREEN HILL   Mountain in Hitachi Province, according to early sources

FORMER REGENT   *See* Konoe Michitsugu

FORMER TAKATSUKASA REGENT FUYUHIRA   *See* Takatsukasa Fuyuhira

FORMER TŌ MAJOR COUNSELOR   *See* Nijō Tameyo

FUDANKŌJI   Temple located on Ninth Avenue in Kyōto

FUJIWARA NO HIDEMUNE (mid-twelfth century)   Father of Fujiwara no Hidetō and Hideyasu

FUJIWARA NO HIDETŌ (1184–1240)   Name also read Hideyoshi; also known by his Buddhist name, Nyogan. Served in the personal bodyguard of Go-Toba and was a very active poet in the latter's salon

FUJIWARA NO HIDEYASU (precise dates unknown)   Older brother of Fujiwara no Hidetō

FUJIWARA NO IETAKA (1158–1237)   Major poet and member of Retired Emperor Go-Toba's salon who was highly regarded by Teika

FUJIWARA NO KANEFUSA (1001–1069)   Courtier poet of the *Goshūishū* era

FUJIWARA NO KANEMUNE (1163–1242)   Son of Tadachika

FUJIWARA NO KINTŌ (966–1041)   Poet and scholar of the mid-Heian period. Author of *Waka kuhon*

FUJIWARA NO MICHITOSHI (1047–1099)   Prominent poet and compiler of *Goshūishū*

FUJIWARA NO MICHITSUNE (mid-twelfth century)   Governor of Izumi Province

FUJIWARA NO MOROZANE (1042–1101)   Regent, poet, and patron of the arts

FUJIWARA NO MOTOTŌ   *See* Saitō Mototō

FUJIWARA NO MOTOYO   *See* Saitō Motoyo

FUJIWARA MUNEMOTO (precise dates unknown)   Also known as Genshō. Son of Motoyoshi (Poem 93)

FUJIWARA NO MUNEYUKI   *See* Hamuro Muneyuki

FUJIWARA NO NOBUNARI (b. 1197)   Son of Chikakane

FUJIWARA NO NOBUZANE (1177–1265)   Major poet and painter of the Shinkokin era

FUJIWARA NO SANEKUNI (1140–1183)   Poet and expert on the Japanese flute (*fue*)

FUJIWARA NO SANESADA (d. 1191)   One of Fujiwara no Shunzei's nephews

FUJIWARA NO SANEYORI (900–970)   Critic and major poet in both Chinese and Japanese

FUJIWARA NO SHUNZEI (1114–1204)   Major poet, scholar, and critic. Founder of the Mikohidari poetic house

FUJIWARA NO TAMEIE (1198–1275)   Son and heir of Fujiwara no Teika. Poet, scholar, and critic. Sole compiler of *Shoku gosenshū* and one of the compilers of *Shoku kokinshū*

FUJIWARA NO TAMENORI (1227–1279)   Son of Tameie. Founder of the Kyōgoku lineage

FUJIWARA NO TAMEUJI (1222–1286)   Oldest son of Fujiwara no Tameie. Senior member of the Mikohidari lineage (Poem 64)

FUJIWARA NO TEIKA (1162–1241)   Poet and scholar regarded with his father, Shunzei, as founder of the medieval poetic tradition. One of the compilers of *Shin kokinshū* and sole compiler of *Shin chokusenshū*

FUJIWARA NO TOSHIKOTO (d. 1325)   Son of Nijō Tameyo's

younger brother, Tamekoto. Older brother of Tamemoto, who was adopted into the Kyōgoku house as Tamekane's heir. Adherent of the Kyōgoku faction

FUJIWARA NO YOSHIFUSA (804–872)   Major political figure of the early Heian period

FUKAKUSA   A place in the Fushimi area, south of Kyōto

FUYUHIRA   *See* Takatsukasa Fuyuhira

GISHŪMON'IN NO TANGO (precise dates unknown)   Daughter of Minamoto no Yoriyuki. In service to Empress Ninshi, daughter of Fujiwara no Kanezane

GLOOMY MOUNTAIN   *See* Utsunoyama

GO-KYŌGOKU LORD   *See* Kujō Yoshitsune

GO-SAGA IN   *See* Retired Emperor Go-Saga

GO-SAIONJI LAY-MONK CHANCELLOR   *See* Saionji Sanekane

GO-SHŌNEN IN   *See* Takatsukasa Fuyuhira

GO-TOKUDAIJI MINISTER OF THE LEFT SANESADA   *See* Fujiwara no Sanesada

GYŌKŌ (1391–1455)   Descendant of Tonna. Prominent poet of the early fifteenth century

HAFURIBE TADANARI (precise dates unknown)   Son of Chikanari. Priest at Hie Shrine

HAFURIBE YUKIUJI (precise dates unknown)   Son of Yukikoto. Priest at Hie Shrine

HAGIWARA PALACE   Primary residence of Retired Emperor Hanazono

HAMURO MITSUCHIKA (1176–1221)   Son of Mitsumasa

HAMURO MUNEYUKI (1175–1221)   Courtier in service of Retired Emperor Go-Toba. Executed for his role in the Shokyū Rebellion

HIDEMUNE   *See* Fujiwara no Hidemune

HIDEYASU   *See* Fujiwara no Hideyasu

HIDEYOSHI   *See* Fujiwara no Hidetō

HIGASHIYAMA   *See* Eastern Hills

HIROSAWA   Pond in northern Saga, just outside Kyōto to the west

HITOMARO   *See* Kakinomoto no Hitomaro

HIYOSHI SHRINE   Shintō shrine in Ōtsu, on the shore of Lake Biwa, in ancient Ōmi Province

HŌGAN KENYO (precise dates unknown)

HŌRIN   Hōrinji, a temple in Saga, just outside Kyōto to the west

HOSSHŌJI   Pure Land temple in the Eastern Hills of Kyōto

ICHIJŌ DHARMA SIGN   *See* Jō'i

ICHIJŌ KANEYOSHI (1402–1481)   Statesman poet

IETAKA   *See* Fujiwara no Ietaka

IMADEGAWA'IN KONOE NO TSUBONE (precise dates unknown)   Daughter of Takatsukasa Korehira (b. 1199), who served Kishi, a consort of Emperor Kameyama

IMAGAWA RYŌSHUN (1326–1420?)   Head of major military house and connoisseur of the arts. Partisan of the Reizei lineage and teacher of Shōtetsu

JAKU'E (precise dates unknown)   Also known as Junkyō and Shun'e. A ying-yang master in Kamakura who was a confidant of Prince Munetaka and active in poetic circles there. Later, a student of Fujiwara no Tameie and his son, Tameuji. Friend of Tonna (Poem 89)

JAKUREN (d. 1202)   Lay name, Fujiwara no Sadanaga. Nephew of Fujiwara no Shunzei. One of the major poets of the Shinkokin age. After beginning a career at court as foster son of Shunzei, he took the tonsure around 1172

JIEN (1155–1225)   Also known as Jichin. Son of Fujiwara no Tadamichi and younger brother of Fujiwara no Kanezane. Chief priest of the Tendai sect. Major Shinkokin-era poet and patron

JINGOJI   Shingon temple in Takao

JISSHŌ HŌ'IN (precise dates unknown)   Son of Chōshun. Librarian in the Poetry Bureau during the compilation of *Shoku goshūishū*

JITSU'I (1223–1281)   Son of Takatsukasa Korehira. Major Archbishop

JŌBEN HŌ'IN (b. 1256?)   Like Tonna, a disciple of Nijō Tameyo who became known as one of Four Deva Kings of Poetry (Poems 33, 52)

JŌ'I (d. 1326?)   Name also read Sadatame. Son of Nijō Tameuji and half brother of Tameyo. Known as Ichijō Hō'in and Daigoji Hō'in

JŌSHŌ   *See* Nakamikado Tsunetsugu

JUNKYŌ   *See* Jaku'e

JUST-SO BRIDGE   *See* Mama no Tsugibashi

KAJII PRINCE OF THE SECOND RANK   *See* Son'in Hōshinnō

KAJUJI   Shingon temple complex at Yamashina, in the Eastern Hills of Kyōto

KAKINOMOTO HITOMARO (fl. ca. 680-700)   Poet of the Man'yō era

KAKUDŌ SHŌNIN (precise dates unknown)   Son of Takatsukasa Korehira

KAKUJO HŌSHINNŌ (1247–1336)   Son of Emperor Go-Saga. Abbot of Shōgo'in cloister who also served as head priest of Onjōji and Tennōji. Patron of Tonna and other Nijō poets

KAKUYO HŌSHINNŌ (1320–1382)   Son of Emperor Hanazono

KAMO NO MASAHIRA (d. 1176)   Poet of the *Kin'yōshū* era

KAMO NO UJIHISA (mid-Kamakura period)   Married his daughter to Nijō Tameyo

KAN'E   *See* Chōshun

KANEMORI   *See* Taira no Kanemori

KANEMUNE   *See* Fujiwara no Kanemune

KANEUJI *See* Minamoto no Kaneuji

KANGAKU'IN One of the buildings of the Imperial University, located just north of Third Avenue in Kyōto

KATANO MOOR Moorlands in Kawachi Province along the shore of the Yodo River, famous as a hunting site

KEIUN HŌ'IN (precise dates unknown) Son of Jōben. Priest at Shoren'in Temple. One of the Four Deva Kings of Poetry (Poem 14)

KEIYŪ HŌGAN (precise dates unknown) One of Fujiwara no Tameie's sons. Affiliated with Ninnaji. Librarian in the Poetry Bureau during the compilation of *Shoku shūishū*

KENKŌ (b. 1283) Major poet of the Nijō school and one of Tonna's cohorts. Author of *Tsurezuregusa* (Essays in idleness) (Poem 27)

KENSHŌ (1130–1209) Adopted son of Rokujō Akisuke. The Rokujō house was one of the major poetic houses of the late Heian and early Kamakura periods. Rival of the Mikohidari house

KENSHUN (1299–1357) Son of Hino Toshimitsu. Major Archbishop in the Shingon sect, abbot of Daigo Sanbō'in, and chief priest of Tōji. One of closest advisers and confidants of Ashikaga Takauji

KEN'YO (1275–1325) Appointed Major Archbishop in 1319. Priest in one of the cloisters of Ninnaji, near Tonna's cottage (Poem 79)

KI NO TSURAYUKI (ca. 872–945) Scholar, poet, and one of the compilers of *Kokinshū*

KIN'O *See* Ogura Kin'o

KINTŌ *See* Fujiwara no Kintō

KITABATAKE CHIKAFUSA (1293–1354) Scholar and poet of the Murakami Genji line. Partisan of the Southern Court and author of *Jinnō Shōtōki* (A record of gods and sovereigns) (Poem 11)

KITABATAKE TOMOYUKI (1290–1332) Son of Moroyuki. Middle Counselor of the Second Rank. Adherent of the Southern Court (Poem 67)

KITANO SHRINE Prominent Shintō shrine, located at the western end of First Avenue in Kyōto

KONOE MICHITSUGU (1333–1387) Regent and patron of poets

KONRENJI Time temple in Kyōto

KORETSUGU *See* Taira no Koretsugu

KOREYORI *See* Ōimikado Koreyori

KŌSEN Identity unknown

KUJŌ OF THE SECOND RANK *See* Kujō Takanori

KUJŌ TAKANORI (1269–1348) Kyōgoku poet

KUJŌ TSUNENORI (1331–1400?) Son of Michinori. Regent and patron. Confidant of Shogun Ashikaga Yoshimitsu

KUJŌ YOSHITSUNE (1169–1206) Regent, poet, and patron

KUNIFUYU *See* Tsumori Kunifuyu

KUNISUKE *See* Tsumori Kunisuke

KUNIMI SHINNŌ (1302–1375) Son of Emperor Go-Nijō. Patron of both Tonna and Kenkō

KYŌGOKU LAY-MONK MIDDLE COUNSELOR *See* Fujiwara no Teika

KYŌGOKU TAMEKANE (1254–1332) Son of Fujiwara no Tamenori and grandson of Tameie. Leader of a powerful poetic faction allied with the Jimyō'in lineage of the imperial family

KYŌKEN (precise dates unknown) Son and heir of Tonna

LAKE BIWA Lake in Ōmi Province, north of Kyōto. Also known as the Sea of Grebes

LAY-MONK FORMER CHANCELLOR *See* Tōin Kinkata

LAY-MONK NOBUZANE *See* Fujiwara no Nobuzane

LAY-MONK MINISTER OF POPULAR AFFAIRS *See* Fujiwara no Tameie

LAY-MONK PRINCE OF THE SECOND RANK *See* Son'in Hōshinnō

LORD AKIIE *See* Rokujō Akiie

LORD ENKŌ'IN *See* Takatsukasa Mototaka

LORD KANEUJI *See* Minamoto no Kaneuji

LORD KORESUKE *See* Taira no Koresuke

LORD MITSUCHIKA *See* Hamuro Mitsuchika

LORD MASAYORI *See* Asukai Masayori

LORD MUNEYUKI *See* Hamuro Muneyuki

LORD NOBUZANE *See* Fujiwara no Nobuzane

LORD OSHINOKŌJI *See* Nijō Michihira

LORD TAKANORI *See* Kujō Takanori

LORD TOMOIE *See* Rokujō Tomoie

MAJOR COUNSELOR KANEMUNE *See* Fujiwara no Kanemune

MAJOR COUNSELOR KOREHIRA *See* Takatsukasa Korehira

MAMA NO TSUGIBASHI Poetic landmark in ancient Shimōsa Province

MANO MOOR Moorlands on the coast of the Inland Sea, near modern-day Kōbe

MASTER TAMESADA *See* Nijō Tamesada

MEETING HILL *See* Ausaka

MIBU, MIBU OF THE SECOND RANK *See* Fujiwara no Ietaka

MIBU NO TADAMINE (tenth century) Major poet of the *Kokinshū* era

MICHINARI *See* Minamoto no Michinari

MICHITSUNE *See* Fujiwara no Michitsune

MIDDLE COUNSELOR TAMEHIDE *See* Reizei Tamehide

MIHARU ARISUKE (precise dates unknown) Courtier poet of the *Kokinshū* era

MIKOHIDARI LAY-MONK AND MAJOR COUNSELOR *See* Nijō Tamesada

MIKOHIDARI MAJOR COUNSELOR *See* Nijō Tamesada

MINAMOTO MAJOR COUNSELOR *See* Kitabatake Chikafusa

MINAMOTO MIDDLE COUNSELOR *See* Kitabatake Tomoyuki

MINAMOTO NO IENAGA (d. 1234) Poet and librarian during the compilation of *Shin kokinshū*

MINAMOTO NO KANEUJI (d. ca. 1278) Librarian in the Poetry Bureau

MINAMOTO NO MICHINARI (d. 1019) Contemporary of Nōin and Fujiwara no Nagatō

MINAMOTO NO MITSUYUKI (1163–1244) Prominent poet and scholar of *Genji monogatari*

MINAMOTO NO MUNEUJI (d. 1329) Son of Minamoto no Mitsunobu

MINAMOTO NO SANEAKIRA (910–970) Courtier poet

MINAMOTO NO SHUNRAI (1055–1129) Son of Tsunenobu (1016–1097). Prominent court poet whose poems were greatly admired by Shunzei and later Mikohidari poets

MINAMOTO NO SUKEMICHI (1005–1060) Musician and court poet

MINASE OF THE THIRD RANK (d. 1262?) *See* Fujiwara Nobunari

MINISTER OF POPULAR AFFAIRS *See* Nijō Tamefuji

MINOR CAPTAIN TAMENORI *See* Fujiwara no Tamenori

MITSUCHIKA *See* Hamuro Mitsuchika

MITSUTOSHI *See* Hamuro Mitsutoshi

MIYOSHI AKIHISA Identity unknown (Poem 93)

MONGAKU SHŌNIN (precise dates unknown) Priest of the Shingon sect of the late Heian and early Kamakura periods. Active in the political conflicts that led to the Genpei Wars of 1180 to 1185. Known for his physical prowess

MORU MOUNTAIN Poetic landmark in ancient Ōmi Province

MOUNT FUJI Most famous of Japanese mountains, located in the Hakone area, southwest of Kamakura

MOUNT KŌYA Mountain in Kii Province. Site of the Shingon Kongōbuji temple complex

MOUNT HATSUSE Mountain in Yamato Province, near modern-day Sakurai City. Site of a famous temple dedicated to Kannon

MOUNT TAKANO *See* Mount Kōya

MUNEYUKI *See* Fujiwara no Muneyuki.

MUSHANOKŌJI SANEKAGE (1661–1738) Major poet and critic of the mid-Edo period

MUSHŌ (late Kamakura period) Prominent *renga* master

NACHI WATERFALL Famous poetic landmark at Kumano, in Kii Province

NAKANO'IN One of the residences of Fujiwara no Tameie, located in

Saga, just west of Kyōto. Deeded to him by his father-in-law, Utsno-miya Yoritsuna

NAGAHIDE   *See* Nakajō Nagahide

NAKAJŌ NAGAHIDE (precise dates unknown)   Also known by his Buddhist name, Gen'i. Hyōgo Lay-Monk and warrior poet who was probably one of Tonna's poetic disciples (Poem 43)

NAKAMIKADO   *See* Nakamikado Tsunetsugu

NAKAMIKADO TSUNETSUGU (1258–1326)   Founder of the Nakami-kado lineage. Major Counselor of the Senior First Rank before tak-ing the tonsure in 1326

NAKAZONO LAY-MONK CHANCELLOR   *See* To'in Kinkata

NIJŌ CONSULTANT   *See* Nijō Tametada

NIJŌ LAY-MONK AND MAJOR COUNSELOR   *See* Nijō Tameyo

NIJŌ MICHIHIRA (1287–1335)   Regent and father of Nijō Yoshimoto

NIJŌ NORISADA   *See* Asukai Norisada

NIJŌ TAMEAKIRA (1295–1364)   Son of Nijō Tamefuji. Designated compiler of *Shin Shūishū* but died before it was completed. Tonna was appointed to complete the project in his stead

NIJŌ TAMEFUJI (1275–1324)   Son of Tameyo. One of Tonna's teach-ers and patrons. Designated chief compiler of *Shoku goshūishū* (Later collection of gleanings continued, 1325), which was completed by his nephew Tamesada after Tamefuji's sudden death (Poems 16, 45, 47, 49, 51, 53, 58, 88, 118)

NIJŌ TAMESADA (1293–1360)   Grandson of Nijō Tameyo. One of Tonna's primary patrons. Chief compiler of *Shin senzaishū* (New col-lection of a thousand years, 1360) (Poems 42, 54, 56, 77, 80, 85, 101)

NIJŌ TAMETADA (d. 1373)   Son of Tamefuji. Allied himself with the Southern Court at the time of Go-Daigo's rebellion, but later re-turned to the Northern Court, around 1351

NIJŌ TAMEYO (1250–1338)   Blood-heir of Fujiwara no Teika. Head of the Nijō poetic house, leader of the most powerful poetic faction at the imperial court, and Tonna's teacher. Sole compiler of *Shin gosen-shū* (New later collection, 1303) and one of the compilers of *Shoku senzaishū* (Collection of a thousand years continued, 1318–1320) (Po-ems 3, 37, 44, 50)

NIJŌ YOSHIMOTO (1320–1388)   High-ranking courtier and major poet and critic. One of Tonna's patrons (Poems 99, 115)

NINNAJI   Shingon temple in modern-day Omuro, Kyōto. Tonna's Saike'en cottage was located within the temple's vicinity

NOBUZANE   *See* Fujiwara no Nobuzane

NŌYO (precise dates unknown)   Poet. Contemporary of Tonna

OBATADA   Also read Owarida. Site believed to be in ancient Settsu Province

ŌE NO HIROMOTO (1148–1225)   Scholar, courtier, and government official in the Kamakura shogunate

OGURA CONSULTANT MIDDLE CAPTAIN   *See* Ogura Sanena

OGURA KIN'O (thirteenth century)   Courtier and Middle Counselor. Founder of Ogura lineage

OGURA LAY-MONK MAJOR COUNSELOR   *See* Ogura Sanenori

OGURA SANENA (1315–1404)   Grandson of Ogura Kin'o. Courtier poet (Poems 34, 131)

OGURA SANENORI (1264–1349)   Son of Ogura Kin'o. One of Tonna's confidants

ŌMIDŌ   An area in Kamakura, just west of the Shakadō Valley

ONO NO KOMACHI (mid-ninth century)   Female poet

ŌSHIKŌCHI NO MITSUNE (d. ca. 925?)   Prominent poet of the *Kokinshū* era

POETRY BUREAU   Court bureau used primarily for the processes involved in putting together an imperial anthology

POSTHUMOUS THIRD RANK   *See* Tameko

PRINCE MOTOYOSHI (890–943)   Poet of the *Kokinshū* era

REGENT   *See* Nijō Yoshimoto

REIZEI   One of the residences of Fujiwara no Tameie, located near Reizei Avenue in Kyōto

REIZEI CONSULTANT   *See* Reizei Tamehide

REIZEI MAJOR COUNSELOR   *See* Fujiwara no Tameuji

REIZEI TAMEHIDE (d. 1372)   Second son of Tamesuke, founder of the Reizei line of the Mikohidari house. One of the compilers of *Fūgashū* and a sometime confidant of Tonna (Poems 98, 126, 132)

REN'A (precise dates unknown)   Lay name, Kuno Saburō (Poem 98)

RENCHI   *See* Utsunomiya Sadayasu

RETIRED EMPEROR FUSHIMI (1265–1317)   One of the emperors of the Jimyō'in lineage. Student of Tamekane and supporter of the Kyōgoku faction

RETIRED EMPEROR GO-FUSHIMI (1288–1336)   Son of Fushimi

RETIRED EMPEROR GO-NIJŌ (1285–1308)   Son of Go-Uda

RETIRED EMPEROR GO-SAGA (1220–1272)   Kunihito, eighty-eighth Emperor of Japan. Son of Tsuchimikado. Served as Retired Emperor during the reigns of Go-Fukakusa and Kameyama

RETIRED EMPEROR GO-UDA (1267–1324)   Partisan of the Nijō house. Issued the order for compilation of *Shin gosenshū*

RETIRED EMPEROR HANAZONO (1297–1348)   Student of Kyōgoku Tamekane and a support of the Kyōgoku faction. Issued the order for compilation of *Fūgashū*

RETIRED EMPEROR KAMEYAMA (1249–1305)   Partisan of Nijō house. Issued the order for the compilation of *Shoku shūishū*

RETIRED EMPEROR KŌGON (1313–1364)   One of the emperors of the Jimyō'in lineage

REVEREND JICHIN   *See* Jien

ROKUJŌ AKIIE (1153–1223)   Prominent poet

ROKUJŌ [CHIGUSA] ARIFUSA (1251–1319)   Major poet, scholar, and calligrapher. Partisan of the Daikakuji imperial lineage

ROKUJŌ TOMOIE (1182–1258)   Poet of the Shinkokin era. Student of Teika who later allied himself with Shinkan in defiance of Teika's son, Tameie

ROKUJŌ YUKIIE (1223–1275)   Son of Tomoie. Member of the anti-Mikohidari faction led by Shinkan

RYŪSHIN SHŌNIN   *See* Enkū

SAGA   Area west of the capital. Site of the villa of Fujiwara no Teika and his heir, Tameie

SAIGYŌ (1118–1190)   One of the most important of all classical poets. Close friend of Shunzei

SAIONJI SANEKANE (1249–1332)   Important court political figure and patron

SAISHŌ TENJI (precise dates unknown)   Name also read Saishō Na-ishi no Suke. Daughter of Asukai Masaari (1241–1301) and wife of Nijō Tamemichi (1271–1299) and later of Retired Emperor Go-Uda. Prominent poet

SAITŌ MOTOTŌ (precise dates unknown)   Contemporary of Tonna who was active in Nijō poetic circles. Records indicate that he served as a steward in the Gate Guards and as an official in the shogunal military offices at Rokuhara ni Kyōto. The Saitō clan was descended from Fujiwara no Uona (721–783) of the northern Fujiwara, and in official documents family members favored the older affiliation

SAITŌ MOTOYO (precise dates unknown)   Son of Saitō Motonaga and brother of Mototō

SAKI NO CHŪGU NO KAZUSA (early twelfth century)   Lady-in-waiting at the time of Emperor Horikawa

SANETŌ   *See* Sanjō Sanetō

SANJŌ SANETŌ (d. 1338)   Middle Counselor at court

SASAKINO SUKEMASA (precise dates unknown)   Sukemasa of the Junior Third Rank. Courtier of the Uda Genji lineage, descended from Michiie (d. 1167)

SEA OF GREBES   *See* Lake Biwa

SEIKAKU (1167–1235)   Son of Chōken. Resident of Ankyō'in, north of the capital. Like his father, known as a talented preacher

SEIKANJI   Shingon temple in the Eastern Hills of Kyōto

SEMIMARA (tenth century)   Legendary recluse

SENSHI NAISHINNŌ (964–1035)   Daughter of Emperor Murakami. Kamo Virgin

SHIGA   Site of an ancient capital on the southern shore of Lake Biwa

SHIICHI SHŌNIN (precise dates unknown)   Priest of the Pure Land sect. Founder of Kaijōji temple in Kii Province

SHIKI NO MIKO (d. 716)   Son of Emperor Tenji (626–671)

SHINGEN SHŌNIN   Identity unknown

SHINKAN (1203–1276)   Lay name, Hamuro Mitsutoshi. Courtier in service of Retired Emperor Juntoku. Exiled to Kyushu for his role in the Shokyū Rebellion, but later pardoned. Courtier and disciple of Fujiwara no Teika. After Teika's death, he found himself at odds with Tameie. One of the compilers of *Shoku kokinshū*

SHŌGO'IN PRINCE OF THE SECOND RANK   *See* Kakujō

SHŌJŌ   Identity unknown

SHŌMYŌ (1112–1187)   Lay name, Fujiwara no Chikashige. Courtier poet

SHŌREN'IN   Tendai temple at Awataguchi, in the Eastern Hills of Kyōto

SHŌSHŌ NO NAISHI (precise dates unknown)   One of the daughters of Fujiwara no Nobuzane

SHUN'E (1113–1191)   Son of Toshiyori. Prominent poet of the generation of Saigyō and Shunzei

SHUN'E   *See* Junkyō

SHUNZEI   *See* Fujiwara no Shunzei

SŌHEKIMON'IN SHŌSHŌ (precise dates unknown)   One of the daughters of Fujiwara no Nobuzane

SONE NO YOSHITADA (fl. ca. 980–1000)   Prominent poet of the Heian era

SON'IN HŌSHINNŌ (1306–1359)   Son of Emperor Go-Fushimi. Head priest of Kajii cloister. Patron of Tonna and Kenkō (Poems 104, 108, 121)

SŌRINJI   Tendai temple in Makuzugahara, Kyōto

SOSEI (precise dates unknown)   Prominent poet of the *Kokinshū* era

SUGAWARA NO MICHIZANE (845–903)   Scholar and statesman poet

SUKEMASA OF THE THIRD RANK   *See* Sasakino Sukemasa

SUMIYOSHI SHRINE   Famous Shintō shrine complex in Sakai, on the coast of the inland sea. The god of Sumiyoshi was patron deity of poets

TADAFUSA (d. 1347)   Great-grandson of Emperor Juntoku

TADAMINE   *See* Mibu no Tadamine

TADANARI   *See* Hafuribe Tadanari

TAGO BAY   Bay on the coast of ancient Suruga Province

TAIKAKU (1151–1203)   Priest of the Takashina lineage

TAIRA MIDDLE COUNSELOR   *See* Taira no Koresuke

TAIRA NO CHIKAKIYO (twelfth century)   Warrior

TAIRA NO KANEMORI (d. 990)   Prominent poet

TAIRA NO KORESUKE (d. 1330)   Son of Nobusuke. Courtier

TAIRA NO KORETSUGU (1266–1343)   Middle Counselor at court.
Mentioned as an expert in Chinese poetry in section 86 of Kenkō's
Tsurezuregusa

TAKANORI   *See* Kujō Takanori

TAKAO   Area north of Kyōto. Site of the Shingon Jingoji temple

TAKASAGO   Coastal area in Harima Province. Site of a Shintō shrine
famous for its pines, which are "twins" to the Sumiyoshi pines across
the bay

TAKATSUKASA FUYUHIRA (1275–1327)   Regent, poet, and patron

TAKATSUKASA KOREHIRA (1199–1262)   Son of Yorihira. Father of
Korehira, Imadagawa Konoe no Tsubone, and Bishop Jitsu'i. Major
Counselor of the Second Rank

TAKATSUKASA KOREYORI (precise dates unknown)   Son of Ōimi-
kado Korehira. Major Counselor of the Second Rank.

TAKATSUKASA MOTOTADA (1247–1313)   Regent, chancellor, poet,
and patron

TAMATSU ISLE   Island in Waka Bay, Kii Province. Site of a shrine
dedicated to the god of Japanese poetry

TAMEIE   *See* Fujiwara no Tameie

TAMEKANE   *See* Kyōgoku Tamekane

TAMEKO (precise dates unknown)   Daughter of Nijō Tameyo who be-
came consort of Emperor Go-Daigo, giving birth to two of his sons:
Takayoshi and Muneyoshi. Poet

TAMEMUNE   Identity unknown (Poem 93)

TAMENORI   *See* Fujiwara no Tamenori

TAMESADA   *See* Nijō Tamesada

TAMEUJI   *See* Fujiwara no Tameuji

TEIKA   *See* Fujiwara no Teika

TŌ'IN KINKATA (1291–1360)   Foster son of Tamesada. Major political
figure and court scholar. Close ally of the Nijō poetic house who
adopted Nijō Tametō (1341–1381)

TŌJI'IN POSTHUMOUS MINISTER OF THE LEFT   *See* Ashikaga
Takauji

TOKIWAYAMA   *See* Evergreen Hill

TOKI YORIYASU (1318–1387)   Shugo daimyō of Mino and later of Owari
and Ise Provinces. Important warrior figure and patron of poets

TŌ LAY-MONK YUKIUJI (d. 1325)   Warrior who served the Shogun
Prince Munetaka

TŌ MAJOR COUNSELOR   *See* Nijō Tameyo

TŌ NO TSUNEYORI (1402–1484) Warrior poet

TOMINOKŌJI *See* Ogura Sanenori

TOMOIE *See* Rokujō Tomoie

TOMOYUKI *See* Kitabatake Tomoyuki

TŌREN (d. 1182) Monk and poet who was active in the Kairin'en salon

TOSHIKOTO *See* Fujiwara no Toshikoto

TOSHIZANE *See* Bōjō Toshizane

TSUCHIMIKADO'IN KOSAISHŌ (precise dates unknown) Daughter of Fujiwara no Ietaka

TSUMORI KUNIFUYU (1269–1320) Eldest son of Tsumori Kunisuke. Head priest of Sumiyoshi Shrine. His sister was one of Nijō Tameyo's wives

TSUMORI KUNIMOTO (1023–1102) Head priest of Sumiyoshi Shrine and poet

TSUMORI KUNISUKE (1242–1299) Head priest of Sumiyoshi Shrine. Governor of Settsu Province and courtier who went as high as senior fourth rank

UJI Rural area south of Kyōto known for its pastoral beauty. Site of many temples and villas

UJI RIVER River that ran through the Fushimi area, just south of the capital

UNKEN (precise dates unknown) Also known as Raku'a and Raku'ami. Lay name, Budō Tamemochi. Warrior active in poetic circles. One of Tonna's patrons

URABE NAKASUKE Identity unknown

UTSUNOMIYA TŌTŌMI LAY-MONK RENCHI *See* Utsunomiya Sadayasu.

UTSUNOMIYA SADAYASU (precise dates unknown) Son of Utsunomiya Yasumune. Provincial governor and daimyō

UTSUNOYAMA Mountain in Suruga Province

YAMABE NO AKAHITO (early eighth century) Poet of the Man'yō era

YASUKAWA River in Ōmi Province, just east of Kyōto

YOKO MOORS Poetic landmark in Kawachi Province

YORIYASU *See* Toki Yoriyasu

YOSHIAKIRA *See* Ashikaga Yoshiakira

YOSHIDA NO KENKŌ *See* Kenkō

YOSHIDA SPRINGS Spring in the Yoshida area, across the Kamo River to the east of Kyōto

YOSHINO Mountainous area in central and southern Yamato Province. Famous for cherry blossoms and autumn leaves

YOSHINO RIVER River running through the Yoshino Mountains

YUKIIE *See* Rokujō Yukiie

YUKIUJI *See* Hafuribe Yukiuji

Sources of the Poems

Original texts of all the poems translated in this book can be found in volume 4 of *Shimpen Kokka taikan*, ed. Shimpen Kokka Taikan Henshū I'inkai (Tokyo: Kadokawa Shoten, 1986). The numbers correspond to the poems as numbered in that edition. SS refers to *Sōanshū*; ZSS, to *Zoku Sōanshū*.

43.	SS: 861	80.	SS: 1223
44.	SS: 868	81.	SS: 1243
45.	SS: 907	82.	SS: 1247
46.	SS: 913	83.	SS: 1249
47.	SS: 924	84.	SS: 1252
48.	SS: 927	85.	SS: 1255
49.	SS: 930	86.	SS: 1259
50.	SS: 941	87.	SS: 1264
51.	SS: 942	88.	SS: 1285
52.	SS: 943	89.	SS: 1299
53.	SS: 964	90.	SS: 1336
54.	SS: 971	91.	SS: 1341
55.	SS: 973	92.	SS: 1354
56.	SS: 976	93.	SS: 1359
57.	SS: 979	94.	SS: 1365
58.	SS: 988	95.	ZSS: 24
59.	SS: 1004	96.	ZSS: 65
60.	SS: 1006	97.	ZSS: 69.
61.	SS: 1014	98.	ZSS: 72.
62.	SS: 1032	99.	ZSS: 79
63.	SS: 1033	100.	ZSS: 90
64.	SS: 1042	101.	ZSS: 99
65.	SS: 1046	102.	ZSS: 111
66.	SS: 1048	103.	ZSS: 135
67.	SS: 1052	104.	ZSS: 138
68.	SS: 1053	105.	ZSS: 161
69.	SS: 1062	106.	ZSS: 164
70.	SS: 1069	107.	ZSS: 169
71.	SS: 1080	108.	ZSS: 180
72.	SS: 1085	109.	ZSS: 191
73.	SS: 1100	110.	ZSS: 196
74.	SS: 1134	111.	ZSS: 217
75.	SS: 1174	112.	ZSS: 241
76.	SS: 1193	113.	ZSS: 262
77.	SS: 1194	114.	ZSS: 275
78.	SS: 1208	115.	ZSS: 285
79.	SS: 1221	116.	ZSS: 288

117.	ZSS: 302	134.	ZSS: 458
118.	ZSS: 311	135.	ZSS: 564
119.	ZSS: 314	136.	ZSS: 568
120.	ZSS: 315	137.	ZSS: 570
121.	ZSS: 330	138.	ZSS: 575
122.	ZSS: 332	139.	ZSS: 580
123.	ZSS: 335	140.	ZSS: 584
124.	ZSS: 339	141.	ZSS: 588
125.	ZSS: 353	142.	ZSS: 615
126.	ZSS: 355	143.	ZSS: 617
127.	ZSS: 357	144.	ZSS: 625
128.	ZSS: 385	145.	ZSS: 635
129.	ZSS: 386	146.	ZSS: 637
130.	ZSS: 410	147.	ZSS: 644.
131.	ZSS: 415	148.	ZSS: 650
132.	ZSS: 418	149.	ZSS: 655
133.	ZSS: 432	150.	ZSS: 659

Index of First Lines

Numbers refer to the pages on which the poems appear.

RENGA

The Zen Master Hakuin: Selected Writings, tr. Philip B. Yampolsky 1971

Chinese Rhyme-Prose: Poems in the Fu Form from the Han and Six Dynasties Periods, tr. Burton Watson. Also in paperback ed. 1971

Kūkai: Major Works, tr. Yoshito S. Hakeda. Also in paperback ed. 1972

The Old Man Who Does as He Pleases: Selections from the Poetry and Prose of Lu Yu, tr. Burton Watson 1973

The Lion's Roar of Queen Śrīmālā, tr. Alex and Hideko Wayman 1974

Courtier and Commoner in Ancient China: Selections from the History of the Former Han by Pan Ku, tr. Burton Watson. Also in paperback ed. 1974

Japanese Literature in Chinese, vol. 1: *Poetry and Prose in Chinese by Japanese Writers of the Early Period*, tr. Burton Watson 1975

Japanese Literature in Chinese, vol. 2: *Poetry and Prose in Chinese by Japanese Writers of the Later Period*, tr. Burton Watson 1976

Scripture of the Lotus Blossom of the Fine Dharma, tr. Leon Hurvitz. Also in paperback ed. 1976

Love Song of the Dark Lord: Jayadeva's Gītagovinda, tr. Barbara Stoler Miller. Also in paperback ed. Cloth ed. includes critical text of the Sanskrit. 1977; rev. ed. 1997

Ryōkan: Zen Monk-Poet of Japan, tr. Burton Watson 1977

Calming the Mind and Discerning the Real: From the Lam rim chen mo of Tsoṇ-kha-pa, tr. Alex Wayman 1978

The Hermit and the Love-Thief: Sanskrit Poems of Bhartrihari and Bilhaṇa, tr. Barbara Stoler Miller 1978

The Lute: Kao Ming's P'i-p'a chi, tr. Jean Mulligan. Also in paperback ed. 1980

A Chronicle of Gods and Sovereigns: Jinnō Shōtōki of Kitabatake Chikafusa, tr. H. Paul Varley 1980

Among the Flowers: The Hua-chien chi, tr. Lois Fusek 1982

Grass Hill: Poems and Prose by the Japanese Monk Gensei, tr. Burton Watson 1983

Doctors, Diviners, and Magicians of Ancient China: Biographies of Fang-shih, tr. Kenneth J. DeWoskin. Also in paperback ed. 1983

Theater of Memory: The Plays of Kālidāsa, ed. Barbara Stoler Miller. Also in paperback ed. 1984

The Columbia Book of Chinese Poetry: From Early Times to the Thirteenth Century, ed. and tr. Burton Watson. Also in paperback ed. 1984

Poems of Love and War: From the Eight Anthologies and the Ten Long Poems of Classical Tamil, tr. A. K. Ramanujan. Also in paperback ed. 1985

The Bhagavad Gita: Krishna's Counsel in Time of War, tr. Barbara Stoler Miller 1986

The Columbia Book of Later Chinese Poetry, ed. and tr. Jonathan Chaves. Also in paperback ed. 1986

The Tso Chuan: Selections from China's Oldest Narrative History, tr. Burton Watson 1989

Waiting for the Wind: Thirty-six Poets of Japan's Late Medieval Age, tr. Steven Carter 1989

Selected Writings of Nichiren, ed. Philip B. Yampolsky 1990

Saigyō, Poems of a Mountain Home, tr. Burton Watson 1990

The Book of Lieh Tzu: A Classic of the Tao, tr. A. C. Graham. Morningside ed. 1990

The Tale of an Anklet: An Epic of South India—The Cilappatikāram of Iḷaṅkō Aṭikaḷ, tr. R. Parthasarathy 1993

Waiting for the Dawn: A Plan for the Prince, tr. and introduction by Wm. Theodore de Bary 1993

Yoshitsune and the Thousand Cherry Trees: A Masterpiece of the Eighteenth-Century Japanese Puppet Theater, tr., annotated, and with introduction by Stanleigh H. Jones, Jr. 1993

The Lotus Sutra, tr. Burton Watson. Also in paperback ed. 1993

The Classic of Changes: A New Translation of the I Ching as Interpreted by Wang Bi, tr. Richard John Lynn 1994

Beyond Spring: Tz'u Poems of the Sung Dynasty, tr. Julie Landau 1994

The Columbia Anthology of Traditional Chinese Literature, ed. Victor H. Mair 1994

Scenes for Mandarins: The Elite Theater of the Ming, tr. Cyril Birch 1995

Letters of Nichiren, ed. Philip B. Yampolsky; tr. Burton Watson et al. 1996

Unforgotten Dreams: Poems by the Zen Monk Shōtetsu, tr. Steven D. Carter 1997

The Vimalakirti Sutra, tr. Burton Watson 1997

Japanese and Chinese Poems to Sing: The Wakan rōei shū, tr. J. Thomas Rimer and Jonathan Chaves 1997

A Tower for the Summer Heat, Li Yu, tr. Patrick Hanan 1998

Traditional Japanese Theater: An Anthology of Plays, Karen Brazell 1998

The Original Analects: Sayings of Confucius and His Successors (0479–0249), E. Bruce Brooks and A. Taeko Brooks 1998

The Classic of the Way and Virtue: A New Translation of the Tao-te ching of Laozi as Interpreted by Wang Bi, tr. Richard John Lynn 1999

The Four Hundred Songs of War and Wisdom: An Anthology of Poems from Classical Tamil, The Puranāṇūru, eds. and trans. George L. Hart and Hank Heifetz 1999

Original Tao: Inward Training (Nei-yeh) and the Foundations of Taoist Mysticism, by Harold D. Roth 1999

Lao Tzu's Tao Te Ching: A Translation of the Startling New Documents Found at Guodian, Robert G. Henricks 2000

The Shorter Columbia Anthology of Traditional Chinese Literature, ed. Victor H. Mair 2000

Mistress and Maid (Jiaohongji) by Meng Chengshun, tr. Cyril Birch 2001

Chikamatsu: Five Late Plays, tr. and ed. C. Andrew Gerstle

The Essential Lotus: Selections from the Lotus Sutra, tr. Burton Watson 2002

Early Modern Japanese Literature: An Anthology, 1600–1900, ed. Haruo Shirane 2002

MODERN ASIAN LITERATURE

Modern Japanese Drama: An Anthology, ed. and tr. Ted. Takaya. Also in paperback ed. 1979

Mask and Sword: Two Plays for the Contemporary Japanese Theater, by Yamazaki Masakazu, tr. J. Thomas Rimer 1980

Yokomitsu Riichi, Modernist, Dennis Keene 1980

Nepali Visions, Nepali Dreams: The Poetry of Laxmiprasad Devkota, tr. David Rubin 1980

Literature of the Hundred Flowers, vol. 1: *Criticism and Polemics,* ed. Hualing Nieh 1981

Literature of the Hundred Flowers, vol. 2: *Poetry and Fiction,* ed. Hualing Nieh 1981

Modern Chinese Stories and Novellas, 1919–1949, ed. Joseph S. M. Lau, C. T. Hsia, and Leo Ou-fan Lee. Also in paperback ed. 1984

A View by the Sea, by Yasuoka Shōtarō, tr. Kären Wigen Lewis 1984

Other Worlds: Arishima Takeo and the Bounds of Modern Japanese Fiction, by Paul Anderer 1984

Selected Poems of Sō Chōngju, tr. with introduction by David R. McCann 1989

The Sting of Life: Four Contemporary Japanese Novelists, by Van C. Gessel 1989

Stories of Osaka Life, by Oda Sakunosuke, tr. Burton Watson 1990

The Bodhisattva, or Samantabhadra, by Ishikawa Jun, tr. with introduction by William Jefferson Tyler 1990

The Travels of Lao Ts'an, by Liu T'ieh-yün, tr. Harold Shadick. Morningside ed. 1990

Three Plays by Kōbō Abe, tr. with introduction by Donald Keene 1993

The Columbia Anthology of Modern Chinese Literature, ed. Joseph S. M. Lau and Howard Goldblatt 1995

Modern Japanese Tanka, ed. and tr. by Makoto Ueda 1996

Masaoka Shiki: Selected Poems, ed. and tr. by Burton Watson 1997

Writing Women in Modern China: An Anthology of Women's Literature from the Early Twentieth Century, ed. and tr. by Amy D. Dooling and Kristina M. Torgeson 1998

American Stories, by Nagai Kafū, tr. Mitsuko Iriye 2000

The Paper Door and Other Stories, by Shiga Naoya, tr. Lane Dunlop 2001

Grass for My Pillow, by Saiichi Maruya, tr. Dennis Keene 2002

STUDIES IN ASIAN CULTURE

The Ōnin War: History of Its Origins and Background, with a Selective Translation of the Chronicle of Ōnin, by H. Paul Varley 1967

Chinese Government in Ming Times: Seven Studies, ed. Charles O. Hucker 1969

The Actors' Analects (Yakusha Rongo), ed. and tr. by Charles J. Dunn and Bungō Torigoe 1969

Self and Society in Ming Thought, by Wm. Theodore de Bary and the Conference on Ming Thought. Also in paperback ed. 1970

A History of Islamic Philosophy, by Majid Fakhry, 2d ed. 1983

Phantasies of a Love Thief: The Caurapañcāśikā Attributed to Bilhaṇa, by Barbara Stoler Miller 1971

Iqbal: Poet-Philosopher of Pakistan, ed. Hafeez Malik 1971

The Golden Tradition: An Anthology of Urdu Poetry, ed. and tr. Ahmed Ali. Also in paperback ed. 1973

Conquerors and Confucians: Aspects of Political Change in Late Yüan China, by John W. Dardess 1973

The Unfolding of Neo-Confucianism, by Wm. Theodore de Bary and the Conference on Seventeenth-Century Chinese Thought. Also in paperback ed. 1975

To Acquire Wisdom: The Way of Wang Yang-ming, by Julia Ching 1976

Gods, Priests, and Warriors: The Bhṛgus of the Mahābhārata, by Robert P. Goldman 1977

Mei Yao-ch'en and the Development of Early Sung Poetry, by Jonathan Chaves 1976

The Legend of Semimaru, Blind Musician of Japan, by Susan Matisoff 1977

Sir Sayyid Ahmad Khan and Muslim Modernization in India and Pakistan, by Hafeez Malik 1980

The Khilafat Movement: Religious Symbolism and Political Mobilization in India, by Gail Minault 1982

The World of K'ung Shang-jen: A Man of Letters in Early Ch'ing China, by Richard Strassberg 1983

The Lotus Boat: The Origins of Chinese Tz'u Poetry in T'ang Popular Culture, by Marsha L. Wagner 1984

Expressions of Self in Chinese Literature, ed. Robert E. Hegel and Richard C. Hessney 1985

Songs for the Bride: Women's Voices and Wedding Rites of Rural India, by W. G. Archer; eds. Barbara Stoler Miller and Mildred Archer 1986

The Confucian Kingship in Korea: Yŏngjo and the Politics of Sagacity, by JaHyun Kim Haboush 1988

COMPANIONS TO ASIAN STUDIES

Approaches to the Oriental Classics, ed. Wm. Theodore de Bary 1959

Early Chinese Literature, by Burton Watson. Also in paperback ed. 1962

Approaches to Asian Civilizations, eds. Wm. Theodore de Bary and Ainslie T. Embree 1964

The Classic Chinese Novel: A Critical Introduction, by C. T. Hsia. Also in paperback ed. 1968

Chinese Lyricism: Shih Poetry from the Second to the Twelfth Century, tr. Burton Watson. Also in paperback ed. 1971

A Syllabus of Indian Civilization, by Leonard A. Gordon and Barbara Stoler Miller 1971

Twentieth-Century Chinese Stories, ed. C. T. Hsia and Joseph S. M. Lau. Also in paperback ed. 1971

A Syllabus of Chinese Civilization, by J. Mason Gentzler, 2d ed. 1972

A Syllabus of Japanese Civilization, by H. Paul Varley, 2d ed. 1972

An Introduction to Chinese Civilization, ed. John Meskill, with the assistance of J. Mason Gentzler 1973

An Introduction to Japanese Civilization, ed. Arthur E. Tiedemann 1974

Ukifune: Love in the Tale of Genji, ed. Andrew Pekarik 1982

The Pleasures of Japanese Literature, by Donald Keene 1988

A Guide to Oriental Classics, eds. Wm. Theodore de Bary and Ainslie T. Embree; 3d edition ed. Amy Vladeck Heinrich, 2 vols. 1989

INTRODUCTION TO ASIAN CIVILIZATIONS

Wm. Theodore de Bary, General Editor

Sources of Japanese Tradition, 1958; paperback ed., 2 vols., 1964. 2d ed., vol. 1,
   2001, compiled by Wm. Theodore de Bary, Donald Keene, George Tanabe,
   and Paul Varley

Sources of Indian Tradition, 1958; paperback ed., 2 vols., 1964. 2d ed., 2 vols., 1988

Sources of Chinese Tradition, 1960, paperback ed., 2 vols., 1964. 2d ed., vol. 1,
   1999, compiled by Wm. Theodore de Bary and Irene Bloom; vol. 2, 2000,
   compiled by Wm. Theodore de Bary and Richard Lufrano

Sources of Korean Tradition, 1997; 2 vols., vol. 1, 1997, compiled by Peter H. Lee
   and Wm. Theodore de Bary; vol. 2, 2001, compiled by Yŏngho Ch'oe,
   Peter H. Lee, and Wm. Theodore de Bary

NEO-CONFUCIAN STUDIES

*Instructions for Practical Living and Other Neo-Confucian Writings by Wang Yang-
   ming,* tr. Wing-tsit Chan 1963

Reflections on Things at Hand: The Neo-Confucian Anthology, comp. Chu Hsi and
   Lü Tsu-ch'ien, tr. Wing-tsit Chan 1967

Self and Society in Ming Thought, by Wm. Theodore de Bary and the Conference
   on Ming Thought. Also in paperback ed. 1970

The Unfolding of Neo-Confucianism, by Wm. Theodore de Bary and the Confer-
   ence on Seventeenth-Century Chinese Thought. Also in paperback ed. 1975

Principle and Practicality: Essays in Neo-Confucianism and Practical Learning, eds.
   Wm. Theodore de Bary and Irene Bloom. Also in paperback ed. 1979

The Syncretic Religion of Lin Chao-en, by Judith A. Berling 1980

The Renewal of Buddhism in China: Chu-hung and the Late Ming Synthesis, by
   Chün-fang Yü 1981

Neo-Confucian Orthodoxy and the Learning of the Mind-and-Heart, by Wm. Theo-
   dore de Bary 1981

Yüan Thought: Chinese Thought and Religion Under the Mongols, eds. Hok-lam
   Chan and Wm. Theodore de Bary 1982

The Liberal Tradition in China, by Wm. Theodore de Bary 1983

The Development and Decline of Chinese Cosmology, by John B. Henderson 1984

The Rise of Neo-Confucianism in Korea, by Wm. Theodore de Bary and JaHyun
   Kim Haboush 1985

Chiao Hung and the Restructuring of Neo-Confucianism in Late Ming, by
   Edward T. Ch'ien 1985

Neo-Confucian Terms Explained: Pei-hsi tzu-i, by Ch'en Ch'un, ed. and trans.
   Wing-tsit Chan 1986

Knowledge Painfully Acquired: K'un-chih chi, by Lo Ch'in-shun, ed. and trans.
   Irene Bloom 1987

To Become a Sage: The Ten Diagrams on Sage Learning, by Yi T'oegye, ed. and
   trans. Michael C. Kalton 1988

The Message of the Mind in Neo-Confucian Thought, by Wm. Theodore de Bary
   1989